find your
EXTRAORDINARY

'This book brims with extraordinary beauty, passion, wisdom and
practical application. Jessica is one of the most inspiring leaders
I have ever known. What makes Jessica such a compelling guide
is that she teaches what she has brilliantly practised and proven in
action. She first found the extraordinary in herself against great
odds, before helping countless others do the same'
Shirzad Chamine, *New York Times* bestselling author of
Positive Intelligence

'It's clear Jessica Herrin has found her extraordinary and is
living proof that a woman can and should dream bigger, live happier
and achieve success on her own terms. I am so inspired by
Jessica and the advice she offers in this book'
Christy Turlington Burns, founder, Every Mother Counts

ABOUT THE AUTHOR

ABOUT THE AUTHOR

Jessica Herrin is CEO/founder of Stella & Dot Family Brands. She has been featured on *Oprah, Today, Undercover Boss* and in *Fortune* and the *Wall Street Journal,* and was included on *Inc.*'s list of top ten female CEOs in 2012. Stella & Dot Family Brands (Stella & Dot, KEEP Collective, and EVER Skincare) consists of more than 50,000 business owners in six countries who have earned over $300 million from running their own flexible businesses, sharing over $1 billion in product sales since 2007. Their celebrity-coveted and award-winning products have been featured in *InStyle, Vogue, Allure, Elle* and *Real Simple.*

find your
EXTRAORDINARY

DREAM BIGGER, LIVE HAPPIER AND
ACHIEVE SUCCESS ON YOUR OWN TERMS

**Waterford City and County
Libraries**

JESSICA HERRIN

PORTFOLIO
PENGUIN

PORTFOLIO PENGUIN

UK | USA | Canada | Ireland | Australia
India | New Zealand | South Africa

Portfolio Penguin is part of the Penguin Random House group of companies
whose addresses can be found at global.penguinrandomhouse.com.

First published in the United States of America by Crown Business 2016
First published in the United Kingdom by Portfolio Penguin 2016
001

Printed in Great Britain by Clays Ltd, St Ives plc

A CIP catalogue record for this book is available from the British Library

ISBN: 978–0–241–25091–4

www.greenpenguin.co.uk

Penguin Random House is committed to a
sustainable future for our business, our readers
and our planet. This book is made from Forest
Stewardship Council® certified paper.

To my father, Larry, for the love that fueled my confidence.
All of the good in me is you.

To my husband, Chad, for the love that filled the holes in my
heart. You are my place in this world.

To my daughters, Charlotte and Tatum, for the unbreakable
love of all loves—the happiness explosion that is motherhood.
You are my heart.

To the tribe of women that I call friends. Without your
extraordinary love and support, I could only be ordinary.

contents

PART THREE
The Best Version of You

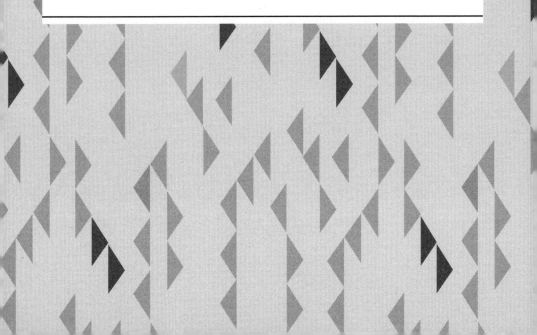

part one

Happiness = Success

say good-bye, ordinary

> Be daring, be different, be impractical, be anything that will assert integrity of purpose and imaginative vision against the play-it-safers, the creatures of the commonplace, the slaves of the ordinary.
> —CECIL BEATON

WHAT IF I TOLD YOU THAT, WITH A LITTLE EFFORT, you could live an extraordinary life? A life in which you felt deep passion for what you did and you always had time for what mattered to you? A life in which you made your most important dreams come true, all while happily leaving behind feelings of inadequacy or guilt, discarding them as if they were corsets from the 19th century?

These days there's a lot of discussion about whether women can have it all. This book isn't about having it all; it's about having what matters most—*to you*. This is a book about achieving your boldest dreams and ambitions, but doing it on *your* terms. I wrote this book to help you find *your* own version of extraordinary—to help you dial up the sound of your own voice so you can tune in to your authentic dreams and develop the will to make them reality.

Now, let's just get this out there . . . it's a tad presumptuous of me to tell other people how to be successful, isn't it? Doesn't it mean I think I'm successful enough to be an expert in the matter? Well, I do consider myself successful, but not for the reasons you might think at first glance.

I've done a lot that I am proud of. I graduated from Stanford, and I've been on the cover of the *New York Times,* called out for being a serial entrepreneur and founder of two successful companies: Della & James, which became WeddingChannel.com, and the company I currently run, the Stella & Dot Family of Brands. And I've had some amazing life experiences—I have been on *Oprah,* I've gone to Buckingham Palace to meet the Queen of England, I've been in the *Wall Street Journal,* and I've had my face broadcast eight stories high in Times Square after ringing the closing bell at NASDAQ for the Stella & Dot Foundation. (That was fun!)

Did sheer luck have something to do with my success? Yes. I was born in the United States, where education is widely available to both genders. I graduated from college in 1994, right around the time women in the United States began earning college degrees in equal numbers with men. Oh—and lest I forget—I went to college in the heart of Silicon Valley right before the commercialization of the Internet and right after the economy recovered from a recession.

Since I sought my first job when the economy was strong, it was easier to take risks, knowing I could always go back and get a safe job. The way society looked at work was changing too. There was a decided shift away from looking at a twenty-five-year tenure at one company and a gold watch at retirement as the pinnacle of success to seeing dropouts and innovators as business heroes.

I was also born into a time when women could play more than menial roles in the workforce. Though our ancestors were around for about six million years, modern humans evolved only about 200,000 years ago. Civilization as we know it is only about 6,000 years old, and industrialization started in earnest only in the 1800s. The 20th century saw the Great Depression, two world wars, and the Vietnam and Korea wars; with all that hardship, women finally began to enter the workforce. (Remember Rosie the Riveter?) But only with the feminist movement of the 1960s did women begin to enter the professional world in great numbers—and we've been gunning to break the glass ceilings ever since.

So, of the 200,000 years in which I could have happened, I was born in 1972 in the United States of America—in the midst of this cultural revolution. I won the lottery of time and place when it comes to women and work.

But it wasn't *just* luck that got me where I am today. In fact, I find it to be true that the harder you work, the luckier you get. And it wasn't just what I was born with, though it's also true that some of my personality traits lend themselves to taking the road less traveled. I would not be where I am if it were not for other skills and characteristics that I've developed along the way. Independence and confidence, passion and drive, decisiveness and tenacity—are all traits of the iconic entrepreneur. In the end, these traits that have made me successful are the ones that you can develop too. They are the habits of mind that allow you to think for yourself and believe in yourself beyond reason; to work hard and find the love in that; to take risks and not be afraid to fail; and to surround yourself with positive people who lift you up. That's the spirit of the entrepreneur in a nutshell. This book will show you how you can find this spirit within yourself.

But my goal is far more ambitious and rewarding than just

showing you how to create a successful company. My goal is to help you create a fulfilling, happy, and successful life—on *your* terms. That's what extraordinary is all about.

I went through times in my life when it looked as if I was successful, but I wasn't really fulfilled or completely happy. Trying to chase *other* people's definition of success instead of your own, I discovered, only looks good on TV. It meant nothing in my own heart and soul.

I see myself as successful today, not because Oprah or the *New York Times* says so, but because I've learned that only *I* decide what success looks like for me. I've learned to believe in myself beyond reason and to forgive myself my many flaws and mistakes. I've boldly jumped into new adventures that I knew nothing about and figured it out as I went. I've learned to stay the course, even when obstacles were in my path and people thought I was crazy. I've given up the guilt about being a working mom, knowing that I am both a great mother and a very busy, very ambitious CEO.

I have learned to push forward into rooms and roles most often held by men without changing the woman that I am. I've learned to work hard on the right things without sacrificing my sanity and my health. Today only I define my success. And only you can define yours.

An ordinary definition of success is making money, moving up the ladder, and being well regarded by others. Extraordinary success, however, includes doing well at something you love and being well regarded by those who matter most to you, especially yourself. It's about learning what you want, developing the confidence to admit it, and having the grit to go out there and get it.

If you are living your life in accordance with your own values and pursuing your own version of happiness, you're being authentic— and that's what leads to success. Success is not about a corporate

Only you
can define
your success.

ladder where the next rung could feel more like a booby prize. One size does not fit all. Happiness doesn't come from success; it *is* success, because if you're happy, then you've succeeded—in the most extraordinary way.

embracing the entrepreneurial spirit

Embracing your entrepreneurial spirit doesn't necessarily mean becoming an entrepreneur. This book is *not* a how-to on starting a company in Silicon Valley (though you might pick up some tips along the way). In fact, I firmly believe that following that path would not make most people happy. That's a good path for calculated risk-loving mavericks who are ultra-intense and somewhat strange—but it isn't the path for everybody. As my sister, Julie, once said to me, in a way only a sibling can, "Don't expect other people to want to do what you do. You're the one that's weird."

When I talk about the spirit of an entrepreneur, I'm describing not just me but anyone who wants to take charge of his or her own life.

Where am I coming from with all of this? Let me first explain a bit more about what I do, and why the vantage point I've gained has given me the insight to write this book. I started a business out of my living room that grew into the Stella & Dot Family of Brands— Stella & Dot, KEEP Collective, and Ever Skincare—which operate in six countries and have empowered over 50,000 independent business owners to embrace their entrepreneurial ambitions *on their own terms.*

Through Stella & Dot, I've focused on changing the lack of

flexibility in the workplace that sidelines too many women as they seek to find a balance between a day job and one of the best jobs—motherhood. Both our Stella & Dot mission and model are designed so that women—and a few good men—can start a business, with very little investment, and choose to run it either part-time to earn extra money or full-time to earn more.

One word lies at the heart of the Stella & Dot mission: *choice.* Everyone has the same start, but everyone chooses their own goals and their own pace. They don't have set hours or sales quotas, and they don't carry inventory or do deliveries. In fact, it's so flexible that 80 percent of our "side-preneurs" operate their business alongside other jobs outside the home.

Being a part of Stella & Dot has allowed me the opportunity to see thousands of wildly different people approach the same opportunity in wildly different ways, producing wildly different results. What I've observed has only strengthened my opinion that it's the individual's will that determines his or her own success, not innate abilities or their past or present circumstances.

When I first started Luxe Jewels (the original name of Stella & Dot), I wanted to do everything I could to help others be successful. So we iterated our product line, our training model, and our sales tools until we thought they were the best they could be. I realized that nothing can ever be perfect, but I wanted to get as close as possible. Several years in, I felt we had done it—created a powerful business platform that worked when you did. In the decade since, our independent business owners have earned more than $300 million in commissions from selling over $1 billion in products.

Yet, I always ask myself: Is there more that we can do? Yes. And that is my motivation for writing this book. I want to help more people cultivate their will, so they are able to create their own way, regardless of their goal. I want to show others how to dig in and figure out their own extraordinary path and discover that to connect "I want" to "I have," you have to be willing to insert "I will" in the middle.

However, though I share many insights from this journey of building the company, this is not a book about Stella & Dot.

Success is not just for someone else.
It is for you.

And let me be clear from the get-go. Even though I am one of the too few female CEOs in Silicon Valley, this is not a discourse about gender equality either. There are other very good books about that! Nor is this a memoir about how I fought the man to get where I am. That was tempting, because these topics sure make for interesting stories. However, *talking* about gender inequality is not how I focus on changing the lot in life of womankind. I have never thought I can do anything a man can do—I have just always thought I can do anything.

So this is a book focused on you and on the fact that *you can do anything*—regardless of the inequalities of the world and your gender.

But to be extraordinary you have to believe that success is not predetermined for the exclusive few. Success is not just for someone else. It is for you.

Creating what you want in your life can happen when you cultivate your entrepreneurial *spirit*. When you develop the will to do things *your* way, without fear of failure or how your choices look to anybody except yourself.

the path to extraordinary

So how will we begin? By tackling the toughest critics we all face—the internal ones. The voice in your head that asks things like "Am I good enough?" and "Do I deserve this?" and "Am I wasting my talents?" and "Are other people judging me?" We'll focus on amping up your self-confidence and positive mind-set so you can have the perseverance to create the extraordinary life you deserve. Call it moxie. Call it grit. Call it right now. You're going to need it.

In the pages ahead, we'll tackle the forces that keep most people from achieving their goals. First, you must have a clear sense of what you want and *why* you want it. It's human nature to lose sight of your goals, to stumble and fall. Do not, however, confuse these setbacks with "I can't do it—it's okay to give up." Once you get clarity on what matters most, you will put that on your "do not quit" list. Then you will go out and make it reality.

Even if you've tried and failed before, have faith! Here's the paradox: as much as getting off track is human nature, so is getting creative and surviving. Ingenuity in the face of adversity is in our blood. Starting from scratch, inventing a tool, using our brains to move forward—that's all encoded in our human DNA. Think about what mankind did to get here. Certainly you can do what it takes to get where *you* want in your life.

Will you have to work hard to get what you want, and will you have to do it despite the odds or obstacles stacked against you? Yes. This book *is* about how *you* can succeed even with the inevitable roadblocks that exist along every road to success, even if that requires you to deviate from the ordinary path.

My path to find my extraordinary has been unconventional. I was a mediocre high school student; I worked my way through community college and found my way to Stanford. I quit my job at the company I cofounded in Silicon Valley to travel the world and follow my husband's career to Texas, so I could start a family. I bootstrapped my second start-up so that I could control the company mission, my destiny, and my schedule around raising my young kids. My journey up to this point hasn't been ordinary—or easy—that's for sure.

Wherever you live, whatever your age or background and whatever your hopes and dreams—whether it's climbing the corporate ladder, starting your own successful business, or being the best damn parent and partner there is—you can use the advice I share in this book to create the life you want.

This book will take you on a journey that will make you feel downright full of yourself. Do you think that's a bad thing? Well, how else are your success and happiness supposed to overflow onto others so that you can nurture them, help them love their lives, and help them find their own strength because you have so much to offer? Being full of yourself is bad only if you are full of crap—saying, doing, and chasing things you don't authentically care about. This book is about just the opposite. It shows you the path to becoming so full of passion, positivity, will, and gratitude that you can transform your life from ordinary to extraordinary— all while you positively impact those around you.

I believe that no matter how you contribute to the world— whether it's by becoming a doctor or a teacher or a stay-at-home mother—your success at whatever you choose is equally important. None of these choices is any less valid than another—they are simply different. The world would be a bizarre dystopia if everyone's value was measured by the same yardstick. We don't all have the same definition of happiness, and thus we don't all have the same definition of success.

And there is no better time than now to ask yourself what really matters to you.

- What makes *you* happy?
- Who are the people you love so much that their joy is your own? What makes them happy? These are the only people you should be trying to impress.
- What do you want your impact to be? And at what scale? Small and personal? Medium or enormous? It's up to you.
- What goal is truly meaningful to you? A career? A steady job and a family? Immersion in your family and your community? You decide what matters most.
- Are you soulfully connected to what you do?

Heavy, I know. But if you don't at first feel conviction in your answers, don't worry—this is just the start of your journey to extraordinary. After all, if you never *ask* the questions, you will never reach the answers.

perfection not required

Hello, Pot. This is Kettle. I'm black, too. You should know right now: I'm not sharing this advice from an ivory tower of perfection. I am *far* from perfect. I make mistakes every day in every area of my life. I just try to learn from them and move on. Isn't that a relief? No one is telling you that to create an extraordinary life, perfection is required. You can start with what you've got, right now, and simply aim to be a bit better every single day. We are all a work in progress.

Plus, I don't adhere to all of this advice all of the time. I just try to follow it most of the time, and more and more over time. Your intention won't always match your actions. Why? You are human. So am I.

you've got what it takes

Okay, so you don't have to be perfect, or gifted from birth. Anyone can do something extraordinary. Do you ever look around at the world, evaluate your life, and see the way you would like it to be instead of the way it is? That's all you need to get started. In fact, that desire to wonder what's possible is what defines your entrepreneurial spirit. You can nurture this side of you into believing you have the power to create change.

All of this capacity within you is what we'll tap into to unleash your entrepreneurial spirit. First you're going to need to believe that confidence comes before competence, failure comes before winning, and happiness comes before success.

Deep down, I think you already know that life is determined not by your past or your circumstances but rather by what you choose to *do* next. The doing is the difference. Your inner kick-ass entrepreneur is all about planning, partnering, and persisting until what you dream and imagine is made real. It's about getting out there and creating success in your life. And I'm talking real success. The kind that puts peace in your mind and happiness in your heart, not just money in your bank account and a title on your résumé. Think that's too much to ask for out of life? It's not.

the six p's of the entrepreneurial spirit

I've boiled the entrepreneurial spirit down to what I call the six P's: Passion + Path + Positivity + People + Perseverance + Productivity. These are the essential tools that will make your goals reachable and your life extraordinary. A lot of people go all passion but with no sense of their path. Passion gives you the gusto to bounce out of bed every morning, but without the path, you will have trouble translating thought into impactful action. Your path is your plan for getting there, at the pace you set.

And no success is possible without cultivating an optimistic perspective—in short, positivity. I am a deep believer in the power of positive thinking. Learning to shift into a positive mind-set helps you dodge the obstacles on your path.

But without the power of people around you to support you, mentor you, and otherwise love you, your passion will fall flat and your plan will never get done. Other people help us make our dreams real, keep us accountable, cheer us on, and make it all worthwhile.

And none of these P's will work if we don't fuel them with perseverance. You'll never hear me say that you can make your dreams come true without hard work. That would be like ocean-front property in Arizona—people may want to buy it, but that doesn't make it real. If you want to be extraordinary, you need to build the resilience to weather the naysayers and develop the determination to reach your goals.

The final P is productivity—how you use your time to make it count, for you. How come something as unsexy as productivity is the last P? Because it is essential if you want to achieve awesome

The 6 p's of an entrepreneurial spirit:

passion

path

positivity

people

perseverance

productivity

things in life without running yourself ragged. Success is about working smarter, not just harder.

You will find practical suggestions that you can apply immediately to your life, including a series of time mastery tips that will rock your crazy, busy world and transform you into an efficiency ninja. Family, work, working out, fun, friendship— yes, they can all coexist, and I'll give you the nitty-gritty on how to get it all done in a day without feeling too stressed or stretched to love your life. I'll show you how extraordinary accomplishment does not have to be at odds with being happy, healthy, and sane. Productivity pulls all of the other P's together and enables you to love your life.

the traits of an entrepreneur

Curious
Freethinking
Imaginative
Confident
Adaptable
Hardworking
Optimistic
Disciplined
Driven
Resourceful
Resilient
Efficient

But I won't sugarcoat it. Because extraordinary isn't for those who think "have it all" means "do it all"—and on someone else's schedule, trying to please all the people all the time. Being extraordinary requires saying no and making trade-offs—a lot.

Together, these six P's are your road map for finding your extraordinary life.

And, I'll share with you how I have stumbled along the way, which is what happens to real people in the real world. I've been successful in business (and life) in spite of major obstacles and mistakes. I have learned to expect these challenges and greet them with good humor! Self-doubt—it's you again! Where have you been? Rejection? I've been wondering when you'd get here. I have your favorite room prepared, but unfortunately, I'll only be able to accommodate you for a *very short* stay.

I'll also share the real stories of many other ordinary people who have done extraordinary things (and you can find pictures and videos of the extraordinary people profiled in this book at www.helloextraordinary.com). You'll see that nobody holds a monopoly over personal struggle. Success happens in spite, not in the absence, of challenge.

By cultivating the six P's, you'll learn to shift your gaze to see the opportunities all around you, instead of focusing on the obstacles. Before we're through, I'll remind you of one of the most powerful coping mechanisms you have at the ready at all times—no matter what—gratitude. And then I'll ask you not only to think about how you can make your own life extraordinary, but to think of yourself as part of a tribe, with an opportunity to make other people happier along the way.

Let's start by asking you some key questions. Pursue the answers to these questions, and you will be on the way to making your one-of-a-kind life extraordinary.

1. What is your PASSION?

2. How do you create a PATH?

3. Do you have a POSITIVE mind-set?

4. Who are the PEOPLE who matter most to you?

5. Are you willing to develop the PERSEVERANCE to outlast your problems?

6. To be more PRODUCTIVE, are you ready to say no to things that don't align with your values and your goals?

You may not know the answers to all of these questions just yet, but don't worry. This process may start messy, but by the end all will be clear as day.

For now, sit back and relax. Enjoy the stories, tune in to your feelings, and trust that by the end of our time together you will have discovered exactly what your version of extraordinary looks like—and how to get there.

So, are you ready? If you aren't going to create what you want in your life, who is? And if you aren't going to do it now, then when?

Let's get started!

believe in yourself beyond reason

I GREW UP IN SCOTTSDALE, ARIZONA, AND WENT TO A Catholic school, Our Lady of Perpetual Help, until the eighth grade. Very strict nuns with rulers, lots of mass in Latin, plaid uniforms, the whole bit. I got an excellent education, including an early degree in Big Catholic Guilt. After I graduated from eighth grade, we moved to Glendale, California, a suburb of Los Angeles. I suddenly went from the most homogeneous school in the world to the most diverse. For over half of the students at my high school, English was a second language.

High school was a blast, but for me, it was also a black hole of learning. Now, this was a three-grade public high school with over 2,000 students. If you were a motivated student, you could get a fine education. If you wanted to skate by, you could do that too. I once had a teacher who handed out the test to our class, then passed around the answer sheet. He was a well-meaning person, but lacked both the necessary resources and training. So yes, skating by was an option.

I was a sporadic student. If interested, I was excellent. If disinterested, I was absent. I was on the student council, the dance team, and the cheerleading squad. I was involved, but I was more focused on socializing than studying. I was on a fast track to being ordinary.

Despite my inconsistent grades, I was placed into AP English, where my teacher, Ms. Carol Irwin, cared more than most. One day when I showed up just as the bell rang, she said, "You're almost late." I replied, "Are you congratulating me? Because almost late is synonymous with on time." To which she replied, "You are out of here!" She was fed up with how many times I was actually late to her fifth-period class and how unprepared I generally was when I sauntered in.

As an indignant youth, I was furious. Sure, my comment was a bit sassy—but kicking me out? Before she sent me down to the principal to request a class reassignment, she called me up to the front of the room. I asked her why she was being so harsh. She gave me a fierce look, shook her head sadly, and in exasperation said, "Because of *you*! I've never seen *such a waste*!"

That was one of the most life-changing compliments and memorable kicks in the ass I'd ever gotten. I knew she was right, and I respected her, even if I didn't show it. I clearly needed the lesson: Did I have talent I was wasting? Was I focused on the wrong things and underinvesting in myself?

Rather than applying myself and actually learning in high school, I was too busy being a moody teen, playing the victim caught up in my mother's bad choices and my parents' dramatic divorce. My parents divorced for the first time when I was in the fourth grade, but there were lots of twists and turns both before and after that happened. Their last separation had come with some surprise impacts on the family finances that affected all of us, but I was most angry with my mom. Though years later I would finally see that my mother was just working with what she had mentally available to her at the time, when I was fifteen, I was less understanding. I felt abandoned and embarrassed by her, and as a result I was angry instead of focused.

Shortly after I was kicked out of the AP English class, I was called to the principal's office again. I thought I was in trouble for skipping another one of my less inspiring classes. I still got mostly A's and B's, but many of my classes were far from challenging and thus not as interesting as going out to lunch with my friends. I waited in the office along with my friend Richie. He too was a bit of a slacker, so finding each other in the principal's office was confirmation that bad news was coming.

Instead, the principal congratulated us for getting the top scores on the SAT pretest you take as juniors, and to our surprise, we were getting National Merit Scholarship Awards. The principal also wanted us to know that we could have letters of commendation sent to two of the colleges we were applying to.

I wasn't sure I was applying to college at all—more like signing up at community college. My sister had just gone off to college, and my dad was already paying that tuition, so money was tight. Plus, with my lackluster GPA, I knew I wasn't going anywhere amazing. Like any seventeen-year-old, I wanted to move out and have all the fun and adventure that comes with going off to college, but would going off with some of my best friends to one of the colleges that would accept me right now be the right choice for me in the long run? Was the quality of education worth the financial strain?

My dad is a brilliant man who has a master's degree in engineering, but he did not travel a conventional educational route in school and thus he never believed in the "top school or bust" philosophy that has only gotten more popular with parents. While he would have made it work if it had been my choice, he was against me applying to a four-year college. His idea was that I should live at home, save money, go to community college, and then transfer. As practical as his plan seemed, I saw this path as a failure, compared to others. I began to wonder what I would be missing out on and how the mistakes I had already made were going to negatively impact my future.

That weekend I went over to my friend's house for a party, since her parents were out of town. Everyone was talking about what colleges they were off to and how excited they were.

There was a paper cutout of a pig with wings dangling from the light fixture over their kitchen table. This Lewis Carroll quote was scrawled on it in pencil:

"The time has come," the Walrus said,
"To talk of many things:
Of shoes—and ships—and sealing-wax—
Of cabbages—and kings—
And why the sea is boiling hot—
And whether pigs have wings."

That poetic gibberish contained a lot of magic for me. Aside from a talking walrus and a bunch of whimsical nonsense, the poem seemed to be telling me that it was time for me to believe that pigs could grow wings, that unreasonable, fantastic things could in fact happen. In that instant, I felt a deep sense of hope and realized that I had to stop wondering what I would be missing out on if I didn't follow the paths of my friends. I had to believe that my own path, starting with community college, might be the best thing that ever happened to me.

I saw clearly that I needed to worry less about how I was failing and wonder more about what I was capable of—and about when and what I was going to do about it. It was as if, in that moment, I realized of course it was not too late to do something bold with my life. I was just going to have to come from behind. I knew that the path I was choosing for myself was not going to be easy or ordinary, but I was going to make it worthwhile.

That moment, I made a decision. I was cracking down and turning things around. I was going to go to community college, seriously bring it, and see where that took me. I was going to stop playing a victim to my circumstances and seeing my future as a product of my past.

That was the first of the many times since in my life when I've come to see that whenever I stop focusing on what I don't have in comparison to others, and just focus on working hard to deserve what I want, I can change my life in the most *extraordinary* ways.

turning it around and cracking down

So I enrolled in Glendale Community College in 1990, the summer I graduated. What was I waiting for? I had a lot of catching up and saving up to do. I took a full course load and worked 20 hours a week waiting tables as well as filing at a law firm.

Those who go straight to a four-year school may think community college is not as hard. That is not the case. Some of the teachers I had there, like Stephen White in economics, were better teachers, in my opinion, than some of the most prestigious professors I had later at Stanford.

There are also those who think community college is full of slackers. That is actually only half true. Classes were a lot less crowded after the first few sessions because some students dropped out, many with the excuse that they were too busy or couldn't afford it. Yet, many others remained there, proving that getting an education was something so important, it could be done alongside putting meals on the table, but only with extraordinary effort. In those classrooms, I met immigrant parents, like one father of three who took an 8:00 AM econ class, rushed out to get to his job as a janitor, then went to a second job, and finally came back to school for the 8:00 PM accounting class. I met many single mothers who worked odd jobs, cared for multiple kids, and earned their degrees at night. I met people who were the utter *opposite* of slackers.

And it wasn't easy competition. Especially in Glendale during that time, the classrooms were filled with adults who had degrees in other countries but were getting recredentialed in the United States. My math and science classrooms in particular were filled with Armenian doctors and engineers. The sheer will and grand diversity of these students taught me two things: brilliant people are everywhere and look a million different ways, and success has many different starts.

To do my best, I would go to the free tutoring center, where I would get help on the subjects I needed to spend extra time on to get an A. I remember one tutor in particular who helped me on a daily basis. I would walk in every day and sit at her table. "Hello, it's me again, your best customer!"

After taking Macroeconomics 101, I fell in love with the subject. Gone was the tardy, class-ditching loser. I was now the eager beaver who highlighted all the extra suggested readings and sat in the front row. Transformation complete. After reading Milton Friedman's book *Free to Choose,* I looked up where the Nobel Prize–winning economist was spending his time. He was a fellow at the Hoover Institution, a leading economic think tank at Stanford University. Most of my friends at the time were awestruck by the celebrities who walked around LA. I was never that impressed.

I wanted to meet Milton Friedman. I started doing more research and found that Stanford had the best undergraduate economics program in the country. Now I had a destination, and I was just beginning to tap into a deep reservoir of belief in myself that allowed me to think I could actually get there.

I was also the best customer of the community college financial aid and guidance counselor's office. If there was a grant, loan, scholarship—you name it—I applied for it. If there was something to know about transfer requirements and applications, I was making an appointment to discuss it.

I went to the transfer counselor to ask how to get an application. After all, Stanford didn't have a website because the commercial Internet did not yet exist! When I told her I wanted to apply to Stanford, she laughed at me. "Why would you apply? That's not reasonable. You would never get in." "But I have straight A's, and I'll get great test scores," I objected.

She replied, "Do you know how many 4.0 students *don't* get in? You don't have a chance. They just don't have that kind of transfer program. No one from Glendale College would get into Stanford!" More chortling and laughing. In my face.

I may sound like a punk here, but in that key moment, when I could have so easily given up on my bold dream, I did not doubt me—I doubted her. I just said something like, "Listen, lady, no one is going to get in if you keep telling them not to apply. If you have such disdain for the students here, perhaps you should seek employment elsewhere. I don't like my tax dollars and tuition funding your bad attitude. I'll ask someone interested in doing their job!" and marched out.

She may have been right that I was a long shot by any objective measure. But she was wrong not to end that little pep talk with,

"Hey, you never know. It can't hurt to try. You just might be the first."

I learned a valuable life lesson right there and then: you have to be your own greatest source of belief and strength. What error would I rather make? Wasting a little time applying or never knowing if I could have been the first student from Glendale Community College to get into Stanford? I could live with being the optimistic fool who applied and didn't get in. What I could not do was be the person who didn't even try.

You have to be your own greatest source of belief and strength.

That same year, 1991, Stanford appointed a new dean of admissions, James Montoya. He was especially keen to explore a previously overlooked source of potential applicants—community colleges—and that year 119 acceptances went out to those coming to Stanford as a sophomore or junior. An unprecedented twenty-three of those went to students from community colleges. Of course, I didn't know any of that the day I got home and found the fat envelope on my pillow.

When I graduated from Stanford in 1994, five years after I was kicked out of Hoover High School Advanced Placement English, I bought the minimum order of announcement cards, even though that cost 200 bucks I didn't have. I bought the cards for one reason: so I could send one as a thank-you note to Ms. Carol Irwin that simply said: "Thank you. I didn't waste it."

I might have sent one to that troll of a guidance counselor at Glendale Community College, too, that simply said: "I told you so!" But I didn't because I had long since forgotten her name. She wasn't worth the space in my brain. Plus, it's far more productive and satisfying to prove the people who believed in you right than it is to prove the people who did not wrong. I forgot her name because I never let that naysayer matter much to me. Naysayers will always crop up in your life. Take care to forget their names as quickly as possible. Don't doubt yourself; doubt the people who doubt you.

I believe I would have been successful regardless of which size envelope I got that day. A school pedigree isn't the key to extraordinary. It's just one thing. If you don't go that way, you just find another route. In fact, if you believe there is only one way to get where you want to go in life, you will never arrive.

The lesson from my entire college experience? If you believe in something enough to be willing to work for it with extraordinary effort, you can make it happen.

a mother lode of confidence

Confidence is not a one-and-done exercise. Are you thinking I'm now going to insist on a Stuart Smalley daily affirmation? Don't worry. To be extraordinary you do not have to look in the mirror and say, "I'm good enough, I'm smart enough, and doggone it, people like me!" But you do have to cultivate your positive mind so you can maintain confidence. Everyone suffers from imposter's syndrome, that feeling that you don't really have what it takes to do what you are doing—and one day soon everyone is going to figure it out! It's not just you who feels that way. And it's okay.

At Stanford, even though I had the confidence to apply, the chops to get in, and the ability to do very well when I got there, I still suffered from imposter's syndrome. But I fell back on one thing I knew about myself: I may not have had the quality of high school education some of the other kids had, but I was going to show up and do my best. I may not have been the smartest kid there, but I was going to try my hardest. Did I fear I wouldn't be top of that class? Definitely. But I also realized I could feel the fear and do it anyway. Another key lesson: you have to push through self-doubt. You have to embrace fear and failure, it's the only way that extraordinary is made real.

confidence boost: ask your younger self what you are capable of

To recharge your confidence, get out a picture of yourself at four or five years old. Describe the person you see in the photo. What do you see in that face? Do you see courage and joy?

What would you tell that child he or she is capable of? What would you want to say to a person who told them they were not good enough? Protect your adult self as you would that child, because that is still you.

I have a 1970s, old-style studio photo of myself from a dance recital at around the age of four or five. I'm wearing a light pink sequined dance outfit, a black top hat, tap shoes, and a cane—and a giant grin from ear to ear.

When I first tried this exercise and looked at this picture, I just started to cry. It was amazing how many mean things I had said to this girl between then and now. Yet in looking at this photograph, all the flaws I think of myself as having suddenly disappeared. When I looked at the essence of this little kid, I saw no evidence of those "less than" qualities I used to believe were my core traits. What I saw was kindness, love, wonder, curiosity, courage, humor, and excitement. I saw a little person who could do anything.

Life may have added some defensive layers, but as soon as I saw that they weren't actually attached to me, I realized I could undo them. Some of my flaws were real, but they were not my identity.

I only vaguely remember the dance recital. I do know I had missed a lot of the practices and I didn't know the routine. I didn't care. I never worried that the crowd would laugh at me. I just got onstage and started tapping my heart out.

be the fool who tries

To create extraordinary in your life, perfection is not required, but a degree of foolishness is. When I cofounded Della & James, the company that became WeddingChannel.com, I was only twenty-four, so I certainly didn't have it all figured out. Though, ironically, like most people at that stage of their lives, I thought I did. I was all energy and confidence. I look back and attribute much of my early success to being naive—too foolish to realize that I had no business dreaming so big and actually succeeding at what I was doing.

I still vividly remember the moment this dawned on me. When I was in business school, about to drop out to start a company,

Embrace
fear and failure.
It is the only way
that extraordinary
is made real.

my cofounder, Jenny Lefcourt, and I reached out for advice before fundraising meetings. Jenny called on her old boss, a serial entrepreneur I'll call John.

John met us in the Stanford Business School cafeteria, which at the time was a windowless basement. (Nothing like the resort it looks like today!) We offered him a rice bowl in exchange for an hour of his "been there, done that" wisdom. We got the better end of that bargain! We sat down and shared our pitch for an online single-stop wedding gift registry—bringing together all the titans of retail and content in one spot on the Information Superhighway. We were pretty impressed with ourselves. The customer value was clear, and better yet, the proof was all right there in our Excel model. This was going to be huge! What was his advice on negotiating the best terms with venture capitalists for our seed round?

A very amused and cool John sat across from us, leaned back, and said, "Wow. I really envy you. . . . Because you are *so* naive."

This was one of those moments when you're thinking, *Was that a compliment?* Because "thank you" is *not* rolling off your tongue.

John then went on to say, "I admire your inexperience. You look at things for the first time and you see this easy path. You just see one wall ahead of you and you think, okay, I can climb over this wall. I get funding. Done. I can declare victory. But I have been down this path before, so I know that wall is much higher than you think. And instead of looking straight ahead at that one wall, I see it from above, and I know that right after that wall, there is another one, and it's just as high, and then another, and another and another. It looks so daunting to me—I'm too tired to start climbing!"

I stayed silent just a second longer, and then, with great sincerity, I quietly said, "Thank you" knowing that in that moment I had learned more than I had in any classroom on that campus.

Right there and then I made a pact with myself to never let life and experience take away my energy and optimism. I vowed to myself I would rather stay a bit of a naive fool than be someone who was too tired to try.

In fact, with the right entrepreneurial spirit, you can gain enough wisdom to see that you have more choices besides just using brute force to climb over every single one of those many, many walls. If you ask for it, and if you're the kind of person who will return the favor, you'll find people to give you a boost. And sometimes, if you look carefully, there is a door. You can just open it and walk through.

Holding on to your optimism while cultivating your wisdom is an art you can master. We want to think that the road to success is paved with golden bricks, but even Dorothy and the gang encountered creepy flying monkeys along their path to Oz. You will always encounter challenges and setbacks on your journey. But the bold remain steadfastly optimistic and always on the lookout for that hidden doorway—because if you think of any road less traveled as too daunting, you will never even begin the journey to an extraordinary destination.

We did raise money for Della & James—in fact, way too much of it in the irrational exuberance of the dot-com heyday. And John was right, of course. Sure enough, right after we climbed over that wall, there was another one, and another one, and another one. People, products, partners, you name it. But we stayed optimistic, and we outlasted those problems.

Along the way I learned another important lesson: don't take yourself so seriously! It's not such a big deal to look like a fool every now and then. Who cares? Remember, it's better to be the fool who tried than the person too daunted to get started. And don't think the presence of obstacles makes you an idiot for going down a path. You see a problem, you figure out how to solve it. You're creating value that way.

Along the way, you'll encounter plenty of naysayers, which is why you'll need a mother lode of confidence. Often you'll have to believe enough for two. Good people will turn into doubters right before your eyes.

Case in point: when Jenny and I initially got funded, we made a deal with our investor, Doug Mackenzie, then a partner at the venture capital firm of Kleiner, Perkins, Caufield & Byers, that we would get $300,000 up front to fund the business through the summer. Doug told us we'd get the next $700,000—and be in business for good—if we met just one condition: sign up Macy's, the store with the largest bridal business in the United States and part of the retail behemoth Federated Department Stores. *That* was the 800-pound gorilla deal.

We hustled that summer, working day and night, seven days a week, out of a tiny office on University Avenue in Palo Alto. We were in a race against the clock, hiring engineers, building the product and custom demos for every retailer we were meeting with to make our pitch.

Jenny has amazing sales skills. She recalls that the son of the CEO of Crate & Barrel told her he was signing because he couldn't bear to see a grown woman beg any longer. Thanks to our hard work, by summer's end we had not only signed several big retailers, we had a letter of intent signed from Macy's. We were stacking up all the right players and were ready to lock and load on our funding.

As part of his due diligence, while he was on vacation in Hawaii, Doug made a call to confirm the Macy's deal as the last step before wiring us the money we needed for our company to survive. On that call, unbeknownst to us, the Macy's executive broke the news that, unfortunately, because of relationships on the board level, they had to back out. They were going with the only competitor out there.

We agreed to meet with Doug in his office the next week when he returned. We walked into that building knowing that we could be walking out with nothing. Summer was up, our seed money was running out, and we had been told we were not welcome back at business school.

Sure enough, when we went in, there was hemming and hawing about the next round of investment. What if the other deals folded, too? Could it be big enough without Macy's? This was looking risky. I told Doug something like, "Look. You identified risk. Kudos! Because that is how you make money. No risk, no return. If you want low risk, you can buy a government T-bill with an extremely low return. If you want venture returns, then take a risk on us. We are going to build this, with or without Macy's, and we need a partner. And not one that is going to flinch with every inevitable hiccup that comes our way. Are you with us?"

It turned out that he didn't need the contract with Macy's after all to believe in our business. He did need to see entrepreneurs who believed in themselves and the potential of their business so much that they could be successful without it. He wired the money. Had we not had a double dose of confidence that day, my first company might never have come to be. The point is, when trouble comes your way and causes doubt, don't flinch. Dig deeper and be confident enough for two.

Eventually, we merged with the competitor that Macy's had signed up with and changed our name to WeddingChannel.com to bring together the true one-stop shop. What a winding road, but in the end we got the deal. Later, we sold the company to the Knot for $90 million.

While that business was not exactly a home run in venture capital terms, I am most proud that our original idea, the one that continues today as a strong part of the business, is a service that millions of people use and love. Not bad for a warm-up round. I see WeddingChannel.com as a key milestone along my path, one that prepared me for Stella & Dot. Better yet, the experience was further proof that if you believe in yourself, work hard, and inspire others to believe in you, too, you can make the seemingly impossible, possible.

feel the fear and do it anyway

Each year Stella & Dot hosts a national sales conference called "Hoopla" for the independent business owners of each of our brands. For the 2014 Stella & Dot Hoopla in Orlando, we brought together thousands of women to learn, grow, celebrate, and have fun together. We have a theme at each conference, and inspiration is always on the agenda. Our goal is not only to inform but to inspire and help our independent business owners take their confidence to the next level. Why is this our focus? Because people already know how to do something. Come on—there is a how-to video on YouTube for just about anything! It's not the *how* to do it that's missing in most people; it's the confidence and motivation to actually do it.

Hoopla has often been called life-changing because it delivers both the how-to and the inspiration to do. We want our business owners to leave after those few days spent together feeling inspired to achieve more not only in their business but also in everything they do that matters to them in life.

Since the conference is held in the summer, my kids are often in attendance. They've grown up with me at Hoopla. We bring our own DJ, and dancing isn't just for our nightclub party. We use music and dance to mix it up and keep the energy high throughout the business training sessions. (No wonder the dentist convention in the next room over always wanders in and wishes they were with us.) The previous year, my daughter Tatum, fresh from her first hip-hop class, bounded up onstage and busted out her moves, with all the confidence and joy of an eight-year-old. Her older sister, Charlie, stayed back. Like a typical ten-year-old, Charlie was more cautious and concerned about what others would think. And because Charlie believes that she inherited her father's rhythm—or lack thereof—she thinks she's a terrible dancer. She was certain she'd make a fool of herself, so she just watched others having fun.

Yet even as Charlie hung back, she admired how brave her sister was, especially when she began to hear the many compliments Tatum got from those watching her. Most important, she noticed that what people *really* loved about Tatum's dancing wasn't her awesome moves, it was her carefree confidence and joy.

The following year, at our "Shine Bright" Hoopla in Vegas, Charlie asked me if she could set things straight. During my keynote, in front of over 3,000 people, she helped me illustrate what being brave was all about. As she stepped out onstage carrying a microphone, I could see the stiffness in her now-eleven-year-old body—and I could feel my own tighten up with her anxiety as she took a deep breath after what felt like a very long pause.

She looked around wide-eyed, taking in the size of the crowd. Then, in a confident, friendly voice, filled with joy, she boomed, "Hello, everybody!" as she smiled and waved to the crowd. I was just so amazed she was out there; I could barely keep it together.

She walked to the very end of a very long stage and continued: "The brave may not live forever, but the cautious never live at all. I learned that quote from the movie I watched last night with my sister, Tatum, *The Princess Diaries*." She went on to tell the audience how, despite her stage fright, she realized that Stella & Dot was all about being courageous and passionate, about being bold, and about not caring what other people think. So she was there that day to get over her stage fright, and since it was Shine Bright Hoopla, she was going to sing them the song "Bright" by Echosmith.

Her song was the sweetest sound I have ever heard. It was the courage of a giant coming out of this little girl. I knew I had to speak after her, but it was all I could do to keep myself from bawling tears of joy. And I wasn't alone. She brought down the house and there wasn't a dry eye in the room.

Afterward, she told me that in that moment, when she paused, she was looking at the crowd and had become afraid. Then, she just asked herself, *What would Mom do?* That inspired her to find her courage again, right there in the middle of her fear. I have never been so proud. I was proud knowing that my company mission and message was spilling over into the most important job I would ever have, being a mother. I was proud that my daughter Charlie felt the fear and did it anyway.

So next time you feel yourself hanging back, remember that extraordinary exists only outside of your comfort zone. Fear will always be there, but if you push yourself to find it, your courage is there, too. You've got to live brave, or you risk having never lived at all.

how brave are you?

Ask yourself these questions:

WHAT WOULD YOU DO IF FEAR WERE NOT A FACTOR? Have you ever let fear hold you back?

WHO IS ON THE LIST OF PEOPLE YOU ARE TRYING TO IMPRESS? Is it a very short list of the people you love the most? And are you at the very top? Or do you live your life trying to impress other people, even some you don't care all that much about?

DO YOU EMBRACE THE PHILOSOPHY THAT THE ONLY WAY TO FAIL IS TO HAVE NEVER TRIED? Do you see failure as a necessary stepping-stone on the path to greatness?

WHO ARE YOU SHARING YOUR BOLD GOAL WITH? That helps make it real. Who do you think will help keep you accountable? How?

WHAT IS THE FIRST THING YOU ARE GOING TO DO THAT IS DARING, THAT HELPS YOU ACCOMPLISH YOUR GOAL? What small action could you take that would advance you along the path to your goal?

look ahead, not back—you're not going that way anyway

In January 2015, I participated in the Silicon Valley Lead-On Conference for Women. It was a bustling gathering of 4,000 women, and confidence was a hot topic.

After my panel, a woman in her fifties came up to me to thank me for the general optimism I had shared. She was tired of hearing speakers spout the general rhetoric on the disadvantaged position of women, without offering enough focus on hope and progress or tactical tips on how to get ahead. She confided that hearing all that "angry ranting" often made her feel worse about her own prospects for advancement in her career and caused her to lose her confidence.

I acknowledged her reaction, because I've heard that same kind of comment many times before. I also have seen the power of what leaving people with hope can do. Yes, it is true that there are more men in executive positions, but so what? That may be a fact, but you don't have to let it be a factor in your career. Forget about it and get back in there.

The woman then said to me, "I had a mother who really picked me apart when I was a girl. I've been trying to stitch my confidence back together for years."

I had to give her some tough love on that one. "Hold on there," I asked her. "How old are you? The statute of limitations on blaming your parents ran out about thirty years ago."

It's not that I wasn't sympathetic. I have walked many miles in those shoes. But at some point you've got to stop casting yourself as the victim of your story and become the hero. Are the odds against you? Good. Every gambler knows that the long shots are where the money is. Now, I don't like to gamble in Vegas, but I go all in when I'm betting on myself. Just assume you are the exception and bet on yourself. Then get cracking on what it takes to make success happen.

Statistics and circumstances do not define you. Difficult pasts shape us, but they do not have to be a factor in why we succeed or why we fail. Something may be a fact, or a feeling, but it does not have to be a factor. I challenge you to ask yourself this question when you are tempted to believe that you will be negatively impacted by a situation. Is that expectation a fact, a feeling, or a factor?

develop your lone eagle confidence

Irv Grousbeck, the professor of the popular "Entrepreneurial Ventures" course at Stanford Business School, tells his class that entrepreneurs have to be lone eagles. "Remember that eagles don't flock; you only see them one or two at a time."

When I heard this metaphor, it resonated with me. Why? What do lone eagles do? They soar high and nest alone. Just like a lone eagle, to create something new you must fly high enough to get the perspective that allows you to see beyond what exists today and envision what could be tomorrow. And you must be willing to follow your own path rather than just pursue conventional wisdom. This metaphor resonates with me because in my own life I have had to be a lone eagle to succeed.

Lone eagle confidence is not about being a contrarian simply for the sake of being different. It's about the ability to see with that heightened, "soaring" perspective, to play for a longer-term outcome, and to be willing to "nest alone." It's not about deciding to *be* a loner. It's about deciding to *decide* on your own what matters most.

We worry so much about what other people think of us, and yet they just don't actually care that much. They are too busy worrying about what others think of them. You can't always be looking left, right, and up and down for external validation for your choices. You've got to keep your eyes on the prize. Dig deep and figure out what it takes to impress yourself and maybe a small circle of people you care most about—your partner or spouse and your kids.

I can tell you why I love being in my forties. You care about people more, but care less about what they think of you. It's an "impress yourself" decade of your life.

To be a success you know that intelligence, creativity, kindness, and work ethic go a long way. But combine those traits with lone eagle confidence and you'll more quickly discover your true passion and create your own opportunities.

With enough lone eagle confidence, you'll have the courage to pursue your authentic life versus the cookie-cutter version other people have in mind for you. And you'll have the courage to stay the course and not let other people's opinions divert you, especially when the going gets tough.

Lone eagle confidence doesn't mean you don't have doubt or fear. It simply means your confidence ultimately wins out in those moments. Feelings of uncertainty are par for the course. In fact, they are a sign that you're on the right track. Because when you chart new territory, you're going where you haven't been before, perhaps where no one has ever been. So of course you don't know it all!

I firmly believe that everyone can cultivate this unique form of perspective and self-confidence. For me, it developed over time and through some pretty awesome "catch your breath" moments. One of those moments came the day I realized that to start my first company, I had to drop out of Stanford Business School.

After a few years working at a couple of technology start-ups, I decided it was time to go back to graduate school. I wanted to start my own company. I knew that not only would returning to school continue my learning, but I would also have the time to further develop my online gift registry idea. I applied to the program at Stanford because they had the best program for entrepreneurial studies. And, let's face it, the weather is pretty nice.

While my intention was to start a business *after* I graduated, it happened much faster. I met Jenny, my cofounder, within the first few days of school, and we discovered we both had similar ideas.

We entered our blended idea into a business plan competition. By the spring of our first year, one of the judges offered to fund the idea if we would drop out to start it.

Imagine this: I'd worked for years to get into that place, and I'd already racked up student loans that would take me years to pay back. Not to mention the fact that fewer than one out of ten start-ups make it in Silicon Valley. Which fate would ours be? To hedge our bets Jenny and I went to speak to the dean of the business school and asked him: could we return if our start-up failed to gain traction over the summer?

His answer? "If it fails, you're not the type of people we want here."

It was a decision of no return, but it was a no-brainer to me. I didn't go to business school to get a piece of paper. I went to get the knowledge, connections, and credibility to get funding to start a company. If that happened before graduation day, I saw dropping out as an efficiency rather than a risk.

Luckily, not every faculty member felt the way the dean did. We were doing an independent study class to get credit for the work we were doing on our business plan, under the guidance of a professor. When we called him to tell him we had gotten funded and were dropping out to go do it, he said, "Well, then you certainly pass my class!"

My lone eagle dad was similarly impressed. He said to me, "Getting into Stanford Business School—that's pretty good! But dropping out? Wow!" Now he was really proud.

Later, when WeddingChannel.com became a successful company, people often asked if I would go back and get my MBA. I had trouble understanding why people seemed so concerned about this. Why would I go back to take courses like "Formation of New Ventures" when I had already formed a new venture? As it turned out, I did go back, but it was to guest-lecture the case on Stella & Dot.

The only problem I ran into about not having that degree was when my husband and I framed our diplomas and went to hang them on our wall. I didn't like his two compared to my one. Not because I wanted to compete with my husband, but because it was really throwing off my vision for the layout of the wall. I take home décor seriously. So, in place of the MBA diploma I never earned, I framed the patent I hold, along with the other inventors, for the technology behind WeddingChannel.com. It blends right in.

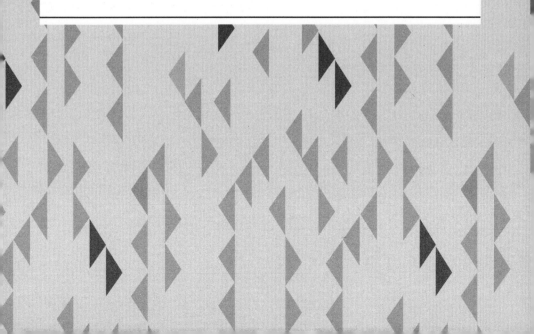

part two

The Six P's of the
Entrepreneurial Spirit

CHAPTER 3

passion

You can only become truly accomplished at something you love. Don't make money your goal. Instead, pursue the things you love doing, and then do them so well that people can't take their eyes off you.

—MAYA ANGELOU

To PURSUE WITHOUT PAUSE OR APOLOGY, ONE true passion, one clear purpose—that is a path to success. But before you go about making your dreams come true, you have to know what your dreams truly are. Discovering your dreams requires an open mind, an open heart, and a willingness to say no. When you hone your entrepreneurial spirit, you are more apt to get those lightbulb moments that guide your extraordinary life.

put your ear down to your heart and listen hard

So what is it that you really want? What is your calling? It sounds lofty and grand, but if you want an extraordinary life, you are going to have to ask yourself those really big questions. To accomplish something really big you have to be pursuing something you truly,

Pursue
without pause
or apology
one true passion,
one clear purpose.

authentically love. Why? Because if it's truly big, getting it done will be harder than you think, and take longer than you want. Only if you love it can you go the distance with joy.

Mark Twain said it best. "There are two very important days in your life. The day you were born, and the day you figure out *why*." When you know what you are passionate about, what you were put on this planet to do, you have found a key first step to living an extraordinary life.

Wouldn't it be nice if you could get a phone call from an oracle? "I have exactly the thing for you! Show up at this address at 10:30 next Tuesday, and *bam!* You'll have passion, joy, and fulfillment dialed in for the rest of your life!" Sorry, it's not going to happen that way. Your passion is going to come unannounced at some uncertain time in the future. For some, the light might go off at twenty years old, thirty-two years old, forty-five, or fifty-eight. And your passion may change as you do. What was right for you in your twenties may not make your heart sing in your thirties, or your forties, and so on.

Are you in a place where you feel like you are not sure which way to go? Which major to pick? Which business concept to pursue? Which career path to follow? Do you have the house, the kids, the spouse, but still feel like you want something more to be excited about? Something just for you? Don't suppress it. Pursue it.

Whatever you choose, make sure you are not doing it solely to win others' approval. Make sure you have a true passion for the life that goes along with it.

I know of no more inspiring story about pursuing a passion to the ends of the earth than that of my business partner, Blythe (Henwood) Harris.

As an art major at Stanford University, Blythe was not sure what to pursue when graduation rolled around—she only knew that she wanted to do something creative and outside of the box. She'd inherited an entrepreneurial spirit from her dad, but as a firstborn child, she also had a strong sense of needing to do something "serious" and achievement-oriented.

While Blythe was wrestling with these two opposing forces, serendipity struck. She met a fellow artist who had an idea for a children's building toy. It was not the most stable opportunity, but it was the one at the intersection of her passions: creativity and entrepreneurship. She didn't know how to make toys, but she was game to figure it out. She pored over books in the library, trying to learn as much as she could about injection-molded plastics manufacturing. Together she and her partner baked prototypes in his oven and refined the design.

They raised some seed capital to support a prototype phase and took the toy they named Zoob to ToyFair to take orders. Two years later, they had $8 million in revenue and outside companies looking to buy them. Beyond just enjoying the success of following her passion to create something from scratch, Blythe learned something really important about herself: yes, she was an artist, but she was also an entrepreneur.

In the years that followed, Blythe dug deep and asked herself what her true passion was and realized she wanted to do accessories design. With some saved money, she moved to San Miguel de Allende, Mexico, to learn metalsmithing and jewelry making. Then, based on the body of work she created there, she was accepted as a visiting artist to the Parsons School of Art and Design in Paris.

While in Paris, Blythe realized that there were no mid-price-point accessories companies that led with great design, and she identified this as a massive market opportunity. There were a lot of options for fine, high-end jewelry, and lots on the low end without great design or quality, but what about the middle? She told herself that she was going to do something on a large scale that reinvented accessible accessories.

She also realized that though she might be a talented designer, she lacked the skills to start and operate a business. So she decided to go back to business school at Columbia University in New York with the goal of learning the tools she needed to go after a business opportunity this ambitious.

After she graduated, she joined the prestigious management training program at LVMH. When she learned that LVMH and DeBeers were launching a business together, she knew it was the opportunity for her. Even though she was told that they were only hiring European-based candidates, that did not deter her. She borrowed miles from her parents and flew to Paris. From the youth hostel where she was staying, she called the CEO and told him she was in town and wanted to meet for coffee. She was a dog with a bone on that opportunity. Passion can do that to you, and you should let it.

Blythe got her meeting with the CEO. Speaking in French, she made her pitch. Her persistence paid off: he said yes, but warned her that he could not pay an expat salary. She didn't care. She knew the role would pay more in experience. To make it work she lived in a 250-square-foot apartment that was so tiny she had to store her bras and underwear in the oven.

The first week on the job she was harassed in every way possible. But she forged on and laughed it off because she didn't care what anybody thought of her. She was going to succeed, and that was all that mattered. And with that attitude, she did. The job turned out to be an incredible training ground where she learned not just how to develop a brand and product line from scratch but also how to thrive in an entrepreneurial culture.

After a few years, she decided it was time to go home to San Francisco and focus on the mid-market accessories opportunity she had dreamed of. She cold-called the head of Banana Republic accessories every week until she got a meeting. Six months later, she had the job of head of jewelry. In one year, she saw the business double from $25 million to $50 million.

What did Blythe do that was so extraordinary? She did the soul searching to find her passion, and then she followed that passion wherever it led her. She was willing to give up things that mattered less (like an apartment with room for drawers) to get things that mattered more. She developed her talents to serve her passion and used them to make something even greater exist. When she followed her passion, it led her to find the extraordinary within herself.

passion has to be personal

When I have had the opportunity to speak at business schools, I often encounter earnest students who come up to me afterward with their pitch. I love young people who are personally connected to and passionate about their ideas. However, I must admit that I also hear a lot of buzzword mumbo-jumbo from people hot on the tail of the next big thing. "We are going to disrupt the Internet of Things in the Cloud," they say. Or, "We're going to triple our valuation in three years." I ask them, "How badly do you want this to exist in this world and why? Who is going to care? Whose life is going to be better? Why is this personal to you?" People who start the conversation talking about things like "disruption" and "market size" rarely have good answers.

You need to be invested personally—not just financially—in what you do if you want to make your life extraordinary. Why was passion doubly important to me as a second-time entrepreneur? Because I'd learned that you can create commercial success and still not be completely fulfilled.

When I was twenty-six, Jenny and I appeared on *Oprah* for Della & James (which became WeddingChannel.com). Oprah shared with the world that we had followed our passion to find our fortune, and our company was now worth over $100 million. Though our segment was short, the exposure brought traffic that crashed our website, and, after, I got random phone calls and emails from people all across the country. Excluding the few creepy callers, the questions were mostly from women, all asking the same question: "How can I start a business and create the success in my life that you have?"

How could I respond? "Go to business school (you'll be in debt with student loans). Raise venture capital (which will involve aiming for a liquidity event on someone else's time frame). Get used to hiring and firing employees, doing the job of seven people, and traveling a lot (in other words, working pretty much every night and weekend). But hey, do all this and the world will see you as an exceptional success!"

The problem was that, while the *Oprah* version of our business *looked* like the American Dream, the path to get there had been a bit of a nightmare. It all looked good from the outside, but I was beginning to realize this was a choice I was going to have to reconsider. I had recently gotten engaged, and I knew that shortly after we got married I wanted to start a family. All the travel and long hours simply weren't going to work for me much longer.

As Jenny and I were wrapping up at WeddingChannel.com, Jenny got pregnant. Post-merger, we were dealing with layoffs, traveling between offices in two cities, and just trying to survive in the very tough market of 2000. The job was stressful to say the least. I remember Jenny having an aggressive discussion in a meeting, then patting her belly and tenderly saying, "That's not for you, baby, just ignore Mommy for a minute."

It was during this time that I talked to a woman who was a cofounder and CEO of another e-commerce company and had just had a baby. I asked her for her best advice on starting a company and a family at the same time. Her advice was short and sweet.

"Don't do it!"

Well, that was encouraging.

There had to be a better answer, a doable way to start and run a business while also starting a family. I knew that so many of the people who had asked me for advice along the way were really just seeking ways to achieve more financial independence and be their own boss. What if we could have that *and* raise a family at the same time? What if I could find a way to democratize entrepreneurship so that more people could be successful in business, on their own terms, without all the costs and risks typically associated with start-ups? Without the around-the-clock commitment? Could I help others experience the joy I'd felt from starting my own business, but without so many of the hardships? Could a more doable way of starting and running a business help create more financial independence for women? Could I create something that could help women make life a bit better for their families?

I was hitting on an idea that resonated deeply with me. It was personal. My mother was someone who had felt deep limitations in her life because of financial dependence. She got pregnant with my older brother when she was a teenager and so entered into her first marriage with just a GED and not a lot of options. Seeing how her life played out has no doubt influenced me to always be fiercely financially independent.

As a result, I have had jobs since I was fifteen and have always saved my own money so I could pay my own way. When I earned money, I invested it to grow my security net. While at community college, I day-traded stock to grow my tuition funds.

Earning and saving money was never about things I wanted to buy; it was more about creating options in my life. I learned early on that, for women especially, money equals freedom of choice.

Sometimes those choices are big ones, such as paying my way through college. And sometimes those choices are less important, for instance, deciding when you can buy yourself something small.

Shortly after my husband, Chad, and I got married, I was working at WeddingChannel.com and supporting us while he was in business school. We were both in the bathroom getting ready for our day when I idly commented, "We need new towels." He looked at the old frayed beach towel hanging on the bar and thought, *Why? These work. These absorb water. Why would we need towels?* (Chad is a typical man who is also against decorative pillows.) He replied, "No, these are great. We don't need towels."

I responded, "Oh, that wasn't a question. More of an FYI. New towels will be appearing here soon. I bring home the bacon, I will decide how I spend $34.99."

While matching towels were not a true need, I have never wanted to be in the position of asking others for purchase approval—even my husband.

Now, while I believe you need to be financially independent so you can make your own choices, I do not believe your choices should be driven solely by money. Money should be a means to live a life you love.

Take the story of my sister, Julie, who was a police officer. When she got pregnant with her first child, she knew she wanted to stay home and care for her daughter. Both she and her husband—also a police officer—were more than willing to make some cutbacks. She has never been materialistic. She was able to take a leave of absence from her job for a year because they had planned ahead and saved for it, but she also knew that living off her savings wasn't a permanent solution.

Looking ahead, she knew that after that year was up she would need to figure out a way to make $1,000 a month if she wanted to keep the family comfortably in their home, in a town with a great school district. Her leave gave her a year to come up with alternative ways to make money.

When Julie was looking for birth announcements for her baby, she noticed there were no options that included color photos. She saw a hole in the market that she could fill, all while working from home and caring for her new baby. So she sold her jet ski and used that money to buy a color laser printer. She bought a book that taught her how to make a website, and she made one. She woke up early to get work done before her family started their day and she continued to work after they went to bed.

Bella Baby Announcements was born the same month as my beautiful niece Lauren.

My sister's passionate desire to stay home with her children drove her success in business. Using the early income she earned from Bella Baby, she was able to grow the business, and by the time she was pregnant with her second child, two years after her daughter was born, she was making enough money that she could resign from the police department. In fact, she was making more money than she'd made as a police officer, working flexibly from home. Her revenue targets were set by how much money she needed to earn to pay her bills without taking another job outside the home. For her, there was no greater mark of success.

Looking back, I have no doubt that watching my sister's tenacity and results helped kindle my passion for focusing on flexible businesses for women. I also often thought *what if my mom had been able to do something like that*? Would that have improved her choices?

But my sister is rather exceptional. Julie's one tough cookie. The time line and investment generally required to start a successful business would daunt most people. Yet, it wasn't just my sister who wanted to earn money on her terms in order to stay home with her kids.

A dual-income household enables flexibility and possibility. Many of our business owners want to contribute to the family finances in order to take the pressure off of a spouse. Oftentimes, that spouse wants to leave a job they don't love in order to pursue a more risky or lesser-paying one that they do.

I also knew that for others, flexible work, seasonal work, and second jobs play a major part of their life plan. People want to pay off debt, work around a school schedule, pay for unexpected expenses like fertility treatments, get a new car, or go on a vacation they could never otherwise afford.

And sometimes, earning your own money isn't really about the money at all. It's about the pride that having an independent income brings. I know a mother of three who loves being home with her kids. Her husband is the primary breadwinner and manages the finances. Each Monday he would lay a couple of $100 bills on the counter as he went off to work—pocket money that she would use for herself and their children that week.

As she grew a part-time business with Stella & Dot, she started earning thousands per month. One weekend, she earned a $750 cash bonus for a promotion. The very next Monday morning, when her husband went to reach for his wallet, she put her hand out like a traffic cop to signal "Stop!" Pulling out her stack of $100 bills, she said, "No thanks, dear. I've got this. But do you need some extra pocket money?" He just looked at her in awe as she stuck a couple of $100 bills in his pocket, gave him a big kiss, and walked out of the kitchen. Now that's priceless!

At WeddingChannel.com, a day came when I realized I had to devise an exit strategy. It wasn't just the intensity of the hours I was working and my life stage that made me move on. It was the intensity of the passion I felt—or rather, didn't feel—for the company mission during those long hours. How much did I really care about weddings? I had loved my own wedding, sure, but beyond that, was this industry a calling for me? Was this work going to be my impact on the world?

Helping women create more choices in their lives, both big and small, is so personal to me—it's my forever passion. When people ask me about my exit strategy for this company, I say, "Oxygen tank and a stretcher."

Are you doing something right now, or pursuing something right now, that you love so much, you wouldn't mind it being the job you retire from? If not, what is stopping you?

I did not have industry experience when I started Stella & Dot. I was pregnant with a full-time job, and the timing was far from perfect. But since I had authentic passion, it trumped everything else. True passion, I believe, is what makes your journey worthwhile.

passion grows from passion

Ironically, my very own sister, whose spirit inspired me, never had any desire to be a Stella & Dot Stylist. Fashion is not her thing. In fact, there are plenty of other women out there who have zero interest in fashion but have a similar need for financial flexibility. I knew that to really have a broader impact, our company needed to expand the types of products we offered so that we could serve people with different passions and interests. We needed to become a family of brands.

Our first expansion was KEEP Collective, our keepsake charm accessories line. That was an obvious extension for us, as we had long wanted to offer a collectible concept that helped people keep what they loved close at hand—jewelry that was more about meaning than fashion. Plus, we anchored KEEP at a very affordable price point to appeal to a wide range of household incomes.

As a leadership team, we also knew that a skincare and beauty line would be a major opportunity to have an impact on lots of people who wanted to sell a product other than accessories. This was going to require new partnerships with new people who shared our passion for the mission of making the workplace more flexible for women, and yet who brought a passion for this product category that was truly their own. I began by adding to our board the industry veteran Leslie Blodgett, who had grown a $500 million beauty company. Leslie helped us build a world-class team that had not only expertise but a deep passion for creating beauty and wellness products.

We started working with industry veteran, Christin Powell, who experienced skin cancer in her twenties. Christin took that as a wake-up call to the links between growing rates of cancer and the unregulated chemicals in consumer beauty products. She couldn't find healthy products, so she cofounded an organic skincare line out of her kitchen called Juice Beauty. Yet she realized that if natural skincare products didn't deliver real results, women would keep seeking products that delivered, even if the ingredients were questionable. So she went on to work with clinical lines like Perricone MD, in the prestige market to continue to try to crack the seemingly impossible problem of creating a line that would be both good for the user and capable of delivering real results.

She helped us establish EVER labs and the very passion-driven EVER science team. It took years (and millions and millions in investment) before we finally had the shockingly good clinical results we were after. We would never have gotten there if it hadn't been a passion project all along the way, not just for me, but for the team that made it happen.

passion has its own eta

If you are always on the lookout, you can spot your passion at the oddest times and in the strangest of places. My first job out of college was at Trilogy Software Development Group, a 40-person start-up in Austin, Texas. It was there that I came up with the idea for my first company, the online wedding gift registry that became Della & James, and later WeddingChannel.com.

The culture at Trilogy was intense, and the small team was very talented. Many of those early Trilogy employees have gone on to found other successful companies. I was surrounded by people who wanted to start companies and whose skills were complementary to mine. I lived on fertile ground for coming up with an idea.

Many of my college friends could not understand why I would

choose to work all the time in Austin, Texas, versus New York or San Francisco, where I could "have more fun"—or at least work on something more interesting than enterprise software. The thing is, for me, that *was* fun. They thought I was crazy when we would go away on a girls' weekend and I'd be reading *Computer Reseller News* instead of *People* magazine. So now you know: I may be into fashion, but in my heart I'm still just a geek who has learned to behave somewhat normally in public.

While I was at Trilogy, I was always trying to think up an idea to start my own company based on all the opportunity that the growing consumer Internet would bring. After all, it was in many ways the golden age for start-ups; AOL dial-up was taking off, and Amazon was just about to get started in a garage in Seattle. The more I kept asking myself what these opportunities would be, the more I became fascinated with consumer e-commerce and content.

What would people buy online first, before high-speed bandwidth came about? What consumer experience was fundamentally broken and could be made easier, faster, and better online?

This was what was running through my mind as I ran on a treadmill at the gym off loop 360 when the idea of an online wedding gift registry came to me. Brides and grooms could still go into a few stores to pick out the wedding gifts they would like, but their guests could skip the mall and just purchase a gift off any list online. Just like Trilogy was doing for computer parts, I could start a company that would aggregate the price and availability of wedding gifts. The Internet could make wedding gift-buying so much easier.

This was it! I was so excited I hopped off the treadmill, ran home, and sketched out the beginnings of the business plan. And even though I didn't actually start the business until two years later, that was the day I realized that ideas can come from the most unlikely places if you have a curious and open mind.

My lightbulb moment for Stella & Dot came five years later, in 2001.

When I was at WeddingChannel.com, I took a business trip to Dallas to meet with Neiman Marcus, one of our customers. After a day of meetings, I entered the grand, historic lobby of my hotel and the energy and buzz in the room made me feel like the 100-year-old building was about to lift off its foundation and shoot to the moon. I stepped into one of the old, tiny elevators and came face-to-face with a gaggle of heavily made-up women, clad in pink. This was an elite group of Mary Kay saleswomen. They showed me the sashes, tiaras, and diamond rings they had just been awarded for being top performers. I had read a case study about Mary Kay in business school and had been so impressed that a forty-five-year-old widow in 1963 had the courage to start her own company.

In that moment, in that elevator, I could feel that the company was about so much more than makeup; it had been an on-ramp into the workforce for these women. Seeing them now in front of me, I was awestruck by their happiness. Clearly, they were basking in the moment. But beyond the recognition and the sparkling diamonds, their work had paid mortgages, put kids through school, built their self-confidence, and created happiness!

It took running into those excited, joyful women to make me realize how much *I* wanted to be in the happiness business. I was also struck by a certain paradox: on the one hand, I was viscerally moved by this company's impact on these women, and yet I still thought direct selling was something for my grandmother's generation, not for me. The whole business model felt outdated. As a woman under thirty, I was completely disconnected from the brand and the sales method of direct selling.

I knew that the modern woman had more interest in running an eBay store or a corner boutique than her mother's Tupperware business. The problem is that if you have to come up with what to sell on your own, then procure or make the product, and then take care of shipping and customer service, you risk losing money or making very little per hour after you add up all that effort.

That moment made a lasting impression on me, setting off a series of questions in my mind. I thought back to the women who had asked me for my best advice after I appeared on *Oprah*. Could the home-based business model of yesterday be reworked to solve the modern woman's dilemma of finding that elusive work-life balance? Could it be used to create flexible income so that the choice between motherhood and a career could be less rigid—or could even disappear entirely?

While I continued to work my day job, I began my research of the direct sales industry and began to wonder how I could bring this new dream to life. With a new approach, one that combined high tech and high touch, could I reinvent this outdated model and make it powerfully modern and more profitable than ever before?

Could I find a calling and turn it into a business? One that would be more missionary than mercenary, more about community than capital, and an important next chapter for women in the workplace?

I had the kernel of the ideas for both of my businesses years before I actually founded the company. The ideas simmered while I researched and reshaped and willed for stars to align. I also knew that even though I wanted to pursue remodeling the home-based business for today's needs, the timing wasn't right yet. So I took a job at Dell Computers, knowing that when I was ready, I would start another business to modernize direct sales. I worked nights and weekends, trying to figure out what product I wanted to launch first. I worked through several bad ideas before I got to a good one. When searching for your passion, you will have to kiss a lot of frogs to find the proverbial Prince Charming.

I investigated family games, then crafting, but finally homed in on jewelry. Jewelry was a big market and had the margins to support paying a rewarding commission. It was also something that would fit everyone, would be easy to ship and store, and could easily be shared by women with each other. I saw successful jewelry companies in direct selling, but none that used e-commerce and offered a modern style and brand.

I N 2003, I had thirteen test trunk shows in three months to prove the idea to myself. In 2004, I legally formed and self-funded Luxe Jewels until I got seed funding in 2005. We reached just over $1 million in sales in 2007. In between doing my first test shows and surpassing $1 million in sales, I had two beautiful baby girls. By October 2007, Blythe (Henwood) Harris joined as our chief creative officer, and we changed the name of the company to Stella & Dot, after our grandmothers.

Before Blythe joined, the company was still just ordinary. But when we combined the innovative sales model with her design skills and vision for the product, we became extraordinary. Together, along with the phenomenal sales leaders who joined our company, we grew from $4 million to $33 million, to $100 million and beyond, landing the company on *Inc.*'s "500 Fastest Growing Companies" list. Much more important, we've since paid out well over $300 million in flexible income to our three sales fields, all working on their own terms.

Some bold decisions and some serendipitous encounters have

redirected the course of my life. But I still don't believe that find-ing your passion happens by chance. If you walk eagerly down the road of life with your eyes wide open to the opportunities around you, eventually you will bump right into your passion. The journey to extraordinary starts there.

ask your future self

When I coach our independent business owners, I often begin by asking them if they want a business that is long-term and strate-gic. If they say yes, then I tell them they have to think long-term and strategic. I tell them they have to define their business as big-ger than the outcome of any one sales event or season and make it stronger than the performance of any one team member.

This is also true about how to get the most out of life. In the daily grind of our lives, we tend to focus on the short term. What job pays the most hourly? What is my title? Is my project proposal appreciated?

In fact, most of our thoughts are consumed by the minutiae of our lives. What's for breakfast? Can I make the 6:00 Spin class? Who fed the dog? What time is school pickup? Is anyone other than me capable of putting a dish inside of the dishwasher? And so on.

It's easy to spend your days answering these small, sometimes irritating questions. But soon days turn into weeks and weeks turn into years. And that's it. That's your life, the sum of those minutes and hours. So don't let them go by without asking bigger questions—the questions that lead you to the answers you need to create a bigger life.

In chapter 8, on time mastery, I'll talk about how critical it is to focus on time horizons to get the right stuff done to accomplish your goal. But first, I want you to think way far out into the future. I learned this phenomenal exercise during a personal development retreat for our executive team in Deer Valley, Utah.

Yes, right here and now, we're going to do a mini-visualization exercise. So I'm going to ask you to go deep for a couple of minutes. While you are reading this, if your mind gets lured away by busy thoughts, that's okay and perfectly normal. When you notice a shift in your attention, simply redirect your thoughts to the exercise. This helps you relax and reach better insights. We're going to ask your future self what you are truly passionate about; we're going to ask what matters most. This may seem a bit touchy-feely, but I've been in Northern California for twenty years, what do you expect? Indulge me, and your own imagination, for a few minutes.

Right now, imagine yourself on a gorgeous day, walking toward a river. You approach the water's edge and board a boat. What does the boat look like? Try to put all your attention on seeing details in your mind and let any other thoughts just pass in and out of your head.

The boat begins to drift down the river. As you float down the river you see reminders of your present life—the places you routinely visit, your job, your house, symbols of the things that are important to you and the things you are aiming for.

As you glide down the river, you realize that this is a river of time. You've sailed past a year. What were your happiest moments in that year? A job promotion? A new relationship? Now you see yourself floating past the next five years. What do you focus in on? What is it that you want to see? Are your financial stresses resolved? Are your relationships changed? Is your faith or your health in a different place? Do you remember the job title or the paycheck or the promotion?

Keep going. It's now ten years, now fifteen. Now twenty. What matters to you now? Soon you've drifted thirty, fifty, or even seventy years down the river, and the boat glides over to a dock.

You get off the boat, walk down the dock, and arrive at a beautiful building. Are you in the city or the country? Is it bustling or quiet? There's an open door, inviting you to step inside. Perhaps this door is in a building in a city with texture, loud noises, and scattered light. Perhaps this door fronts a cottage or small house in the countryside and you smell grass or trees. Imagine a really personal place where you've arrived, a place that feels like it was made just for you.

Inside, you recognize the eyes of the person who greets you. It's you—only older and wiser. You sit down across from your future self. Now, what questions do you want to ask this person, who has decades more wisdom than you do?

What matters most to you?
If you could go back, what choices would you make?
What is it that you want me to know about life?
How should I measure success? Is it a number on an income
 statement? A job title?
Is it hugs, kisses, and laughter? Friendships and community?
What was my impact? My greatest achievement?

What do you imagine *your* future self wanting to tell you?

When something small or short-term is weighing me down, I ask my future self if she cares about this at all. Turns out, she actually cares about a pretty narrow set of things! Family, love, friendship, and impact. If she's not overly worried about a short-term situation, why should I be? When the future me looks back with love, small things never come up.

If you ever feel bogged down or stuck, imagine your future, then look back at your life. Ask your future self what matters most.

pay your dues

When I was working as a waitress to pay my way through college, you never heard me say, "Oh, I am just so passionate about people and the food they eat—that is why I do what I do. I love my work. In fact, here is all my tip money—I'm giving it back." No. When I was paying my way through school, I was not passionate about being a waitress. I knew that when I graduated I would figure out my real passion and have the opportunity to pursue it, but that along the way I was going to pay some dues and work some jobs that were not altogether awesome. For me, waitressing was just a way to pay for books in my early years of college, when I really had few other skills and needed a part-time, seasonal job.

My first job after school wasn't a deep passion either—but it helped me pay back the government for my massive student loans, and, ultimately, gave me the financial freedom to find and focus on my real passion.

We all have jobs or roles in life that may not make us want to bounce out of bed, but we know they are nonetheless important—sometimes necessary—to getting to the next step. Even the job I did after founding my first start-up was a "pay my dues" kind of job. Paying your dues isn't just for the young. It's for anyone who wants to get to a better place.

Don't ever think you are above paying your dues. Extraordinary requires not only pursuing your passions with confidence, tenacity, and determination, but also approaching *everything* you do with courage, zeal, gratitude, and good humor! When you bring a positive, grateful attitude to any task, you get more out of it (and you don't suck your own energy dry complaining about it).

Be willing to wait tables. Or wash windows, or bag groceries, or whatever task is equivalent to washing windows in your desk job world—just do what it takes to get to the next level. Just do something to add value and you'll get value out of it. The more you learn, the more insight you'll have when it is time to go out there and do the thing you truly care about. And trust that your experience and learning, along with a curious and positive mind, will help you see the opportunity that is all around you—that's where your passion will come from.

what are you crossing off your list?

You've got to give up a lot of things in order to get those that matter most. So what are you going to cross off your ever-growing list of to-dos and wants? How do you sort through the array of small and big goals and decide which desires are worth going after and which are not as important? As you sift through it all, think about which goals truly motivate you to work tirelessly and make trade-offs. For instance, I really want to speak another language, play the guitar, paint, and play tennis. Can I put any of those aspirations at the top of my list as passions that I am willing to make trade-offs for? No. Not even close. Being extraordinary involves crossing non-passion pursuits off your list. You can't do all things and be all things to all people all the time. You can do anything, but not everything.

You can't
do all things
and be all things
to all people
all the time.

the unicorn farm is not hiring

Do not confuse passion with fantasy. Living your passion will include doing things you detest doing. Things you are not good at. Things that scare you. Things that bore you. That is because you live in the real world, not on a unicorn farm. Think of it this way. What if you created a life so extraordinary that someone decided to make a movie out of it? Guess what would make that movie interesting? The struggle. Without it, there is no triumph. Never shrink away from the challenging things that your passion requires. Otherwise, you'll be robbing yourself of glory. Whatever that challenge is, the sooner you accept it and stop grousing about it, the better off you will be.

Remember, doing great things requires not only hard work but also shit work. So go ahead and embrace the fact that extraordinary will always involve washing windows. Fantastic . . . now you can clearly see the view.

Extraordinary Passion
- Accept that finding passion is a journey. You stay open and you pursue it. Relentlessly.
- Be willing to be a lone eagle—don't seek constant external validation for your choices.
- Cross some of your interests off your list—free up your mind by accepting that there are things that interest you that you will not pursue. If you're merely interested in something rather than passionate about it, it isn't worth your time.
- Being a malcontent will not help you find passion. It will simply make you unhappy. Instead, focus on investing your time and energy in the things that truly matter. The grass may just be greener where you water it.

....

your path of least regret

And the day came when the risk
to remain tight in a bud was more
painful than the risk it took to
blossom.
—ANAÏS NIN

WHO DO YOU KNOW WHO HAS AN EXTRAORDI-
nary life, someone you admire? What path did they
take to get there? What plans did they make to reach
that destination? Was it a path that could only be taken by them,
to a place that could not be arrived at by any other person, any
other way? That's not very likely to be the case. No matter what
you think your flaws are, no matter your circumstances, there is a
path to success for you. It doesn't matter where your path began.
Regardless of what has come before, today is the first day of the
rest of your life.

Your life is shaped by a series of choices and a bit of happenstance. I have always loved the concept of *serendipity*— good things
happening just by pure chance. I love this word so much that I
used to think that if I ever had a girl I would want to name her
Seren. But then, by happenstance, I met a man by the name of

Herrin, and that plan was out the window. I still do love the idea of good luck, though. Who doesn't?

As lovely as it is, however, luck can't be your strategy for life. You can't chart your path to extraordinary based on luck. You need to plan it. And to make that plan a good one, you need to recognize that it's a winding path that will no doubt present you with a few dead ends, some surprising twists and turns, and plenty of obstacles. There is no certain map. You'll need to simply get started to make your way. You will encounter more than one fork in the road, and you'll need to decide to zig or zag. To do that you will need to continue to build up that inner confidence. You will need hope and patience to reach your destination. Then the path becomes not hard but serendipitous, not grueling and confusing but exciting and full of surprises. If you commit to and believe in yourself, you can trust yourself to keep going and to find your extraordinary.

Let me share a little bit of serendipity that I've encountered along my path.

When I graduated from college, with a mountain of student loans, I came to a fork in the road. Which job should I take? I had a job lined up in New York at an investment bank that would have paid a handsome sum. Plus, it was a very well-respected two-year program that would wrap up with a good reference for business school applications. On a last-minute whim, I took an interview with a software start-up in Austin, Texas. The start-up company was run by some young mavericks. The role, like the company, was largely undefined. They knew that I had to give the investment bank my final decision on Monday, so they flew me straight from Austin to meet the CEO at the airport in Utah, where he was currently skiing.

The cabdriver could read the intense consternation on my

face. Good thing we were not playing poker. He looked at me in the rearview mirror and said, "Darling, what have you got your pretty little head so worried about?" I explained the situation. He responded. "Okay. That's easy. Which job has the best upside to it? Is that extra upside worth the risk of the worst-case scenario if you make that choice?"

The investment banker financial analyst program was well defined. It was two grueling years and a path to a great business school. It paid well and would give me solid finance skills. The upside was predictable. That was not the case with the start-up path. The future of the company was unknown, so it could grow quickly and I could grow with it. My role was less defined, but that also meant I could take on more responsibility. Since the upside was not as defined, it was also not as bounded. Technically, it had greater potential. The worst-case scenario would be losing my job, or not liking it and quitting. I would still have my education and could always go back and get the safe job.

The cabbie was right. Taking the job at the start-up became an easy decision. And one that I have never regretted.

Now, at the time I could make that decision because I was footloose and fancy-free. I was twenty-one and totally unattached. If I had had kids and a mortgage, I might not have made the same decision. When you come to a fork in the road, what you factor into your decisions will depend on where you are on your path. But the framework for choosing the path with the maximum upside, as long as it is worth the risk of the downside, still holds up.

dreams can change when you do: a turning point

In my twenties, being an e-commerce entrepreneur was amazing. If you had asked me then, I would have told you I was living my dreams. But as I grew up, my dreams grew up too. Dreams are a moving target throughout your life.

I followed my passion. I built my skills, and I paid off my student loans. I was successful, but I wanted more. I remember admiring my friends who were doctors. They all seemed to have chosen paths that stemmed from a real calling, and such worthy ones at that. They knew their purpose in life. I also admired my brother, a fireman, and my sister, a police officer. They were heroes, every day. I may have been doing well, but they were doing good. As I progressed through my late twenties, more and more I wanted to be soulfully connected to what I did. I was creating jobs and making gift registries easier for busy brides and wedding-goers everywhere. But was that enough? As I pondered that question, a key word kept coming up for me. *Impact.* What was my impact?

I have heard it said that your life can be divided into three phases: learn (school), earn (climb the ladder), and then return (donations and giving back). I started to realize that I didn't want to chop up my life like that. I never wanted to stop learning and I wanted to be returning along the way.

But, was I ready to make a change and leave the company I had started? Sometime after the WeddingChannel.com merger, I looked around with a sense of finality. The original idea had been to create an aggregated wedding gift registry, and check, it now existed. We had a leading e-commerce site, and the company was successful. It had been four years of hard work that felt like forty.

I now was commuting between our San Francisco and Los Angeles offices most weeks. I was twenty-eight years old. I could have started another company in Silicon Valley, but I had more to think about than my career. I had been married for less than a year, and my new husband had graduated from business school and gotten an offer for his dream job—ironically, back in Austin, Texas, where we first started dating. It was a turning point for us.

Twenty-eight seems very young to me now, but at the time I thought I was getting old. I remember being at my desk around midnight, as I often was, and getting an email with an article that showed a graph of a woman's fertility plummeting as she ages. I forwarded the chart to Chad with a one-sentence subject line: "My eggs are rotting."

Did I really expect him to turn down his job so I could stay at mine, knowing I really wanted to have a baby? At the same time that my love for WeddingChannel.com was waning? Plus, we had already decided that before we became parents we wanted to travel. So what did we do? He graduated and I resigned, and then we took three months to travel around the world. We went scuba diving in the Red Sea in Egypt, experiencing dives so incredible we'll remember them until the day we die. We attended a cooking school in Thailand with the slogan *Our food is guaranteed to make you look pregnant.* We went on safari in Africa, and sailed in Croatia. On the trip we talked a lot about what really mattered to us. Traveling together was one of the best decisions we've ever made. Our dreams were focused on starting a family, and that was an even bigger desire than my dream to start another company.

So, when I landed in Texas, I knew I wasn't just going to launch a new start-up right away. A former board member gave me some sage advice: if I wanted to run or build a large company, I should get some experience actually working at one. To date, I had only worked at tech start-ups. Since we were moving to Austin, that meant going to work for Dell Computers.

That advice sounded reasonable, so I took it. It was certainly an unexpected choice for someone who had just left her Silicon Valley start-up.

When I interviewed, I was asked: why would the "Internet poster child" want to work for Dell? That stung a little, implying that working there would be a huge step back. But I didn't see it that way. First, I knew this could be a valuable chapter of my real-life education. Second, I cared more about having a baby at that point than my career. And third, I just didn't really care what that person thought.

Dell became a continuation of business school for me, particularly in that I learned more about how to manage people on a larger scale. I would not have had exposure to that side of business operations if I had only worked at a "Wild West" start-up.

I was working my day job and chipping away at my business plan when, shortly after my thirtieth birthday, I found out that Chad and I were expecting our first child. Getting pregnant only accelerated my desire to get my new business off the ground. I did not want to be a mother working inflexible corporate hours on someone else's schedule.

Hanging in the cube of one of my coworkers was a quote by Cecil Beaton:

Be daring, be different, be impractical, be anything
that will assert integrity of purpose and imaginative vision
against the play-it-safers, the creatures of the commonplace,
the slaves of the ordinary.

Every day I would read it and find inspiration in that quote.

I began planning how I would turn my maternity leave into an eternity leave by exploring every aspect of the home-based direct-selling business. So, I bought an inexpensive ticket to Boca Raton, Florida, to attend the Direct Sales Association's annual conference.

The first day I checked in, got my badge, and immediately pored over the directory to find people I wanted to learn from. I set about talking to anyone who would sit down with me. I raised my hand in every session, asking about the margins required, the key metrics of success, start-up costs, and lessons learned by other companies.

Sounds great, right? It was *painful*. I was suffering from morning sickness that lasted all day and I had to spend a lot of quality time in the bathroom. I was by myself and totally out of my element. And, a chain-smoking elderly man that had clearly had too much to drink by 10:00 AM hit on me. My only response to that was "Eww! Sir, can't you see I'm pregnant!?" As if that was the only thing wrong with that situation.

I called my husband, exasperated: "What am I doing here? Am I completely crazy?" I almost left early and came home. But then I heard some people talking about their sales field in a way that I thought fundamentally missed the boat on what a modern woman wanted. After all, I was that woman! And it wasn't just that conversation; a lot of what I saw was just ripe for change. So I stayed. I knew that if I didn't learn as much as I could about the industry, it would be harder to change it.

I knew the home-based business could be done differently. But did I *really* want to climb that hill? Why not leverage what I already knew and start a software or e-commerce company? I asked myself: What if I failed? What if it didn't work? As much as I tried to talk myself out of the challenge, I couldn't ignore the more optimistic question. What if it *did* work?

I wanted to make an impact helping women create more financial freedom and choice in their lives. Maybe this new path *was* crazy, but this was it.

After returning home, I gave myself a deadline to pick a product, test it, and make a firm go/no-go decision on whether to start a new type of direct-sales business. It had percolated long enough. I knew if I kept analyzing ideas for appeal, margin, or points of difference, I'd never home in on anything. I had to pick first, perfect later.

I circled around the idea that the accessories business was a good opportunity—high margin, easy to ship—so I enrolled in a night class at the local community college to learn how to make beaded jewelry. I walked out of the very first class exhilarated! This was it.

A month later I convinced Chad to skip our plans for a vacation in Mexico and instead go with me to a bead show in Tucson, Arizona. Why have margaritas on the beach when you can traipse through Holiday Inn hotel rooms converted into bead stores? It was as strange as it sounds, but it was an adventure and we had fun! I still have the binder I carried with me to the show with my design inspirations and my bead checklist.

As crazy as this path seemed, *not* chasing my dreams by staying at Dell and in Texas any longer seemed crazier.

And for all the reasons I found to not start the company, I soon found more and more for why I had to. Right after my daughter was born and I returned to work, the CMO began to call 7:00 AM meetings. To get to work on time, I had to turn yet another nursing time into a pumping time. No thanks. That's when I realized I could no longer be happy with someone else dictating my schedule. I wanted to work, but I needed to be the one to decide *when*.

Plus, now with a baby, we really wanted to be back on the West

Coast, where we could be near our families. So when Charlie was six months old, I resigned and convinced my husband to do the same so we could move back to California. It was time to go home.

you don't have to be perfect to start, you have to start to perfect

Too many people worry about how qualified they have to be to begin on a path. Too many people worry that their circumstances and knowledge don't qualify them for taking the next step. But actually, it's the steps that qualify you. Think of trailblazers who have shown there was a way when others thought there was not. Or those who have set out to explore one frontier and ended up discovering a different continent.

If you look at the backgrounds of all the amazing people in the Stella & Dot, KEEP Collective, and Ever Skincare families, you'll find that they all came to their current paths from *very* different entry points.

They have different professional histories. Some are MDs, PhDs, or MBAs, and some have no formal college education at all. Some women have been unicycle coaches, tap dancers, interior designers, style bloggers, artists, or nurses. Many are in the military or married to someone who serves. We have former teachers, dentists, lawyers, political consultants, and vice presidents of finance. Others have been 911 emergency call takers, parole officers, Dallas Cowboy cheerleaders, members of punk girl bands, and sports radio show hosts. Many have reinvented themselves, many times over.

They grew up in different places. Some came from the Philippines, Saudi Arabia, Switzerland, the United Kingdom, both coasts in North America and everywhere in between. Some have never seen the ocean.

They have a great diversity of interests and accomplishments to their names. Some are members of Mensa, some have run the Boston Marathon, and some have been reality TV show contestants or homecoming queens; one was a Miss Teen USA. They've jumped out of planes, gone dogsledding in Canada or power sailing in Florida, and climbed Mount Everest. They love everything from *Star Wars* to the symphony to playing Texas Hold 'Em—and so much more.

And while they are all different, there does seem to be one thing they have in common. They want to create an extraordinary life for themselves and for those they love. They value being a part of a tribe committed to living a bold and joyful life and lifting each other up.

Can we see a correlation between professional background and success? No. Can we see a relationship between a pedigree and success? No. How about geography? No. Well, then what about age or household income bracket? No and no. What about if they are single or married, or have no children or five children? Nope.

Well, then what do those who are successful have in common? It's as clear as day actually. Those who are successful have a willingness to learn, a positive outlook, a bias toward action, and the ability to make midcourse corrections.

The unending diversity among those who have created their own success within our community seems like proof to me that it's not background or personality or interests that determines whether someone can create success. It's not where you start your path—it's what you decide to do along the way. Success is not a birthright; it's the outcome of attitudes and actions.

Don't for a moment look at someone you admire and assume

that you can't get to where they've gotten because you had a different start in life. And don't think that all paths to extraordinary have the same time line. Success can be created at different paces. Don't think about how your past limits your future, but instead about how your unique past has made you stronger.

you are a beginner
at the beginning

We are *all* beginners at the beginning. That sounds obvious, right? And yet, beginnings are daunting—and even more daunting when you hear all the hype (which, by the way, many have debunked) about having to practice 10,000 hours to become an expert at any one task. Well, I don't know about you, but I don't have that kind of time.

In business, I see too many people giving up on something because they think they can never become an expert, so why bother? I can tell you, I see far more people succeeding because they have focused on believing in themselves rather than being too worried about their lack of expertise to begin. Don't worry about sucking at

---

*It's not where you start your path;
it's what you decide to do
along the way.*

---

something at the beginning. Most people do. Then we get better. The only way to get better is to get started.

Here's another story about a remarkable woman whose path to extraordinary began with a rocky start. This woman married her high school boyfriend and by the age of twenty-four had two children and was living on a dairy farm in rural Ontario, Canada. One day when the children were two years and five months, she found herself crying hysterically over the kitchen sink, recognizing she needed to make a dramatic change because she was not happy in her life.

A few days later she got a catalog in the mail for a candle company that offered people the opportunity to earn money selling their products at home parties. She signed up and got to work. She relied on her mother to babysit as she went out and did 138 parties in five months. She sold a boatload of candles and earned more than she had thought possible. She didn't have a manual for how to get there. She knew she wasn't perfect. (She even lit someone's curtains on fire at one of her parties!) She didn't have a ton of skills on her résumé. But she did have a will of steel. Most important, she had a powerful motivator, a powerful *why* (more on that in a minute): she wanted to create a brighter, more independent, bigger life for herself and her children.

That woman is Danielle Redner, now our VP of global training at Stella & Dot—the woman who has inspired tens of thousands to be extraordinary through her firecracker spirit and inspiring, insightful trainings. Crying over the kitchen sink was the start of what would become for her a successful twenty-plus-year career in direct selling that is still going strong. Danielle can help others get over obstacles because she's been there, she's done that. There is in fact nothing that this woman cannot do. And if she can blaze her trail to extraordinary despite her unlikely beginning, so can you.

it's never too late

I have watched women hesitate to go back to work after taking time off because they worry about being out of the loop and are embarrassed that their age is beyond their title and their pay grade. They worry that they don't understand the latest technology and will look like a dinosaur—or as one woman reentering the workforce said, "I feel like I'm riding in on a horse in a hoop skirt!"

You may feel that way too if you are thinking about changing careers or are reentering the workforce after some time off with kids—as though you are back in the boat of paying your dues. That is okay! Be proud of that, not scared or embarrassed. True, chances are, you may face a bit of a learning curve. But while your employer may have to invest in you a bit more at first and you may even earn a bit less than you'd like at first, your life experience *did* make you more mature and wise. Focus on how you can get your foot in the door, then work hard to advance your position. Trust me, it won't take you nearly as long as you think to catch up.

Our Stella & Dot tech group recently sponsored an intern from the Hackbright Academy, the leading software engineering school for women. The academy, which graduates more female engineers than Stanford and UC Berkeley each year, focuses on helping women change their careers. Our intern had a master's degree in literature and was teaching when her husband's job brought them to California. She got a job in technical recruiting and soon realized she'd rather be the one taking the coding job than just helping fill the positions. She took a step back to move forward in a new direction. She had to work hard and essentially start over, but now she's a web engineer, doing something she loves.

It's never too late.

Use your passion to keep yourself honest: Are you fulfilled? Do you need something more? These are bold questions to ask. Don't be afraid to come up with bold answers. It's never too late to pursue what you don't know and what you passionately want.

lone eagles can be confused with loony birds

Starting my second company—and later our second and third brands in the Stella & Dot family—took at least as much lone eagle confidence as dropping out of business school. It wasn't just that I was stepping way out of my comfort zone to learn a new industry and new skills. It wasn't just the years of hard work.

And it wasn't even the bootstrapping. I had to let go of my concern about how the rest of the world would view my journey in order to pursue ideas I couldn't let go of.

After all, what I was doing looked crazy, sometimes even to me. When I was at a crossroads, when I could have become a serial entrepreneur who did it again the Silicon Valley way, I moved to Texas instead to follow my husband's career, took a job as a middle manager at Dell Computer, and started making jewelry in my living room. Doesn't sound like the next chapter of a success story, does it? But it was for me, because at that point in my life my definition of success was starting a family. And I was planning every step of the way. This time I wanted to swing for the fences. I didn't want to just start another business—I wanted to start a life.

Was I worried about people thinking I was making the wrong choice? Was I worried that I could be making more money doing something else? Was I worried that it wouldn't work? Yes, yes, and yes. But I did it anyway. I was more worried about failing myself by not going after what I really wanted.

Many people stay on a path picked by random chance. Maybe they picked a major at age twenty, or decided to go to grad school because they didn't know what else to do and have been on that track ever since, without ever stopping to think whether it is really the right path for them. And even worse, some of us stay on a path that was picked for us by someone else. How many people are in a career based on a major their parents pushed them into? Life is too short. Don't just keep doing what you're doing without questioning it or you'll end up living someone else's life.

what's your *why?*

Over the years, Danielle Redner, our VP of Training, has become the master at helping others chart their path to success. Her first piece of advice? Understand *why* you want to succeed before worrying about *how* you are going to do it. She knows firsthand that if your *why* is bigger than your fears, you can accomplish anything.

Recently, Danielle decided not to just *tell* people how to accomplish a bold and daring goal, but to *show* them. She has wanted to play the drums as long as she can remember. In the fifth grade, her music teacher insisted that only boys should play the drums. So instead, she was allowed to play the French horn, which she hated—especially the spit valve.

Almost forty years later, a tiny part of her still pined to be a rock 'n' roll drummer. To be happy, she didn't need to be a great drummer, she just wanted to be able to play a song and not suck. So she decided to stop thinking about it and just start playing, giving herself not 10,000 hours but instead just ninety days until she planned to perform a drum solo onstage in front of 3,000 people at Hoopla in Vegas.

She hired a teacher and practiced every single one of those ninety days. But before she even got started, her teacher asked her three key things:

1. Do you know *why* you want to do this?

2. Do you accept that this won't be easy?

3. Are you ready to work?

These are exactly the questions we use to help people advance at Stella & Dot. When you can ask yourself these same questions, you will be more motivated to move yourself along on your path, whatever it is.

Knowing *why* you want to succeed is an absolutely essential component to accomplishing any goal. But sometimes, to figure that out, you have to dig a little below the surface. Danielle's *why* was not *just* to learn how to play "Moves Like Jagger." It was to inspire—and to inspire not just that roomful of Stylists but herself as well. And let's be honest, Danielle still wanted to give the bird to that horrible teacher who lied to her about what girls can't do.

When you know your *why*, you can ask yourself the right questions.

Don't ask, "Do I want to get out of bed at 6:00 AM this morning so I have time to practice for an hour today?" Not really.

Instead ask, "Do I want to move people? Am I willing to do what it takes to deliver a training that is not only powerful and impactful but extremely badass?" Yes.

Ask the right questions, get the right answers, and take the right actions.

Does it feel exciting, scary, or uncomfortable to start something new? Yes to all three! When we ask ourselves to do something new, it involves learning, and learning always feels a bit uncomfortable, even stressful. That's why so many people stick with what they know in life—in jobs, in relationships, in routes to the supermarket. But by putting ourselves out there, we challenge ourselves to continue to grow—and we inspire others to do the same.

are we there yet?

"How much longer until we get there?"

You've heard the road trip plea, and you might often find yourself asking that question on your own road to success. All right already! How long is this journey supposed to take? If only there were road signs that could tell you, 2,093 MILES TO SUCCESS, EXIT 30W. While on your journey to extraordinary, you don't get to know in advance exactly how long it will take you to get there. You will certainly see signs of progress along the way. Celebrate each one, and enjoy the ride!

Let's imagine your fantasy success trajectory on a chart. The line simply points up and to the right with a steep slope, right? You wish. In the real world, this graph looks a bit different—more like art from a four-year-old on an Etch A Sketch. Here's my estimate: I find that most overnight success stories take about seven to ten years. It's never as easy, as direct, or as quick as you want it to be!

The business school case study and press on Stella & Dot talks about our hockey stick growth and how we went from $4 million to $100 million in sales in about three years. That is true . . . but it took four years to get to that first $4 million. And it took me two years before that to ruminate on the idea and build my confidence and conviction to do it (not to mention all the years of learning at WeddingChannel.com before that). I didn't take a paycheck until after we were profitable in 2009, *six years* after my first test trunk shows! So no, success did not exactly happen overnight.

Similarly, some might be tempted to call KEEP Collective, which did well over $45 million in its *first* full year of business, an overnight success. But what they'd be missing is the fact that it took us *ten years* as a company to create the infrastructure and insight that our businesses run on, and it took Blythe several years to design and develop an innovative, modern keepsake charm line we could be proud of. Overnight success? Nope. The path was long, but it was the right one. Taking shortcuts would have gotten us lost.

When you believe success is inevitable, you go the distance. You don't panic when you encounter setbacks because you know that is just what the middle looks like. You are only a failure if you stop and stay there. It may take longer to get to where you want to go. You may not get to go in a straight line. Sometimes you'll take a step forward, and then a step back. You will zig and you will zag. You may have to stop and rest a while. Not every spot will have a clear view of the destination. But remember that all you have to do is keep going, one step at a time, and eventually you will reach your goals.

What happens when you arrive to a place in life you deem successful and when you hold the position you worked so hard for? Do you rest on your laurels? Well no, not if you want to stay there. Success is like personal hygiene; it requires daily maintenance.

bullet train to extraordinary

What if you are not moving along fast enough? Don't get frustrated—get curious and motivated. If you are feeling like your progress is stalled, here are a few tips to kick-start it.

- Don't worry about the pace of others. Within our brands, sometimes our independent business owners want to grow a business quickly, and they often compare themselves to someone who has become successful extraordinarily fast with massive effort. But this path generally only leads to feeling disappointed if they don't get there at the same speed. You are far better off looking at the reasonable averages, aligning your expectations with your realistic effort, and plugging away. You don't have to question your goal, but you may have to question your tactics or pace.

- Track your efforts. Keep a daily log to record the times when you were solely focused on what you needed to do to move your goal forward. Be honest. People tend to overestimate how much they are actually doing toward their goal. Want to achieve more? Do more.

- Read the instructions. You may not need to overthink it or re-invent the wheel. Who has done it before, and how did they do it? Do that too.

- Take a look at your results. Be self-aware without being overly self-critical. Ask a straight shooter with experience for feed-back on your approach. In fact, I will be that straight shooter to get you rolling—if you are too sensitive, you will limit your personal growth.

when life has other plans

Sometimes just when everything in life is great, just when you feel you have found your path to extraordinary, everything changes in an instant through no fault of your own. Take the story of Mike Lohner, our Stella & Dot chairman of the board. Mike always studied hard and worked hard and gave back to his community. By all measures, he had created success in life that he truly deserved. He married his high school sweetheart, attended Stanford Business School, and built a passion-filled career. Mike and his wife, Marcee, had four beautiful children together and enjoyed a wonderful life filled with family, faith, music, laughter, and love. His success extended well beyond business. In fact, Mike is one of the happiest people I know.

Then Marcee suddenly got sick. When their youngest two girls were only seven and nine years old, Marcee was diagnosed with a chronic form of Guillain-Barré syndrome, a vicious disease of the nervous system that rendered her partially paralyzed and in unrelenting pain. At her worst point, her weight dropped to ninety pounds, her speech was slurred, she had double vision, and she was so weak that Mike had to carry her up and down the stairs.

Mike's extraordinary career path suddenly seemed irrelevant. All that mattered was getting his best friend back to health. They sought treatment after treatment, and he made helping her get well his life's mission.

This was right about the time we met. At the same time he was teaching me all there was to know about direct selling, he was also learning how to make school lunches, drive carpools, braid hair, and become the primary caregiver in his home. He stepped up to try to fill the role Marcee had always played—and that was a tall order. Marcee is a super-mom and super-homemaker, a leader both in her church and in her community. She had been the rock behind Mike all those years, enabling his success.

So when Marcee got sick, Mike's life path was completely derailed. Suddenly, success had nothing to do with making quarterly sales targets or running a board meeting and everything to do with helping his wife get better while being there for his children. These circumstances forced Mike to very quickly revise his definition of success, and he did. His proudest moment during this period came when his seven-year-old responded to his attempt to sing a bedtime lullaby (Marcee sang bedtime songs every night, so he continued the tradition) by looking up at him from her bed and saying, "Dad, you're a pretty good mom!"

Mike continued to be the rock for the family, and Marcee's health has slowly improved. Today she has more good days than bad days.

The point is that you may have a path all planned out—you may even feel like you have "arrived" at extraordinary—but sometimes life has other plans. Sometimes external circumstances or painful, inexplicable twists of fate force you to change the path you are on, because they change how you can be happy. Sometimes, in an instant, all the professional success in the world can pale in comparison to the joy you feel from seeing an ill spouse regain her health, or the pride you get from a seven-year-old's smile.

We all face challenges in life, and we don't get to know when they are coming and what they are. Mike had to relinquish his former view of success to stay happy in his new life. He had to be the one to lean on his community instead of playing his usual role of strong provider. Regrouping and finding a new path to happiness in those difficult moments will help you once again discover extraordinary.

patience, grasshopper

Your path to extraordinary will also require patience. You can't just hop on another trail and head in a new direction at the first sign of trouble. That won't get you anywhere faster; it will just get you lost. It may be the case that, like it or not, it just takes nine months to grow a baby.

Take my friend Kim. She wanted and deserved a promotion to senior vice president at the very large bank where she had worked for over seven years. She had thrived there, despite the *Dilbert*-like realities of working at *any* large company. Not only was she ready for the challenge of the promotion, but she wanted the matching raise. Kim had two big *whys*. First, she wanted to tear down her home and build a new one to fit her growing family, and she'd need the raise to pay for it. Second, the way she saw it, if she was going to be a full-time working mom and therefore miss precious moments with her kids during the day, she wanted to make her work as impactful as possible, creating things she was proud of. To her, the SVP title was a meaningful emblem of the kind of career momentum she wanted in the context of the large bank.

Kim knew that her goal was within reach, but also that the position she was going after was very competitive. She didn't check off *every* box they were looking for, but she knew that she was a top candidate and that her employer knew she was eager to grow into the role. As a hiring manager herself, she also knew there was *never* a perfect candidate. So why *not* her? She had exciting ideas on what she wanted to do in this new role and had already begun work on them.

Her path to promotion had actually started years earlier. She knew she was a top performer at her level, but she understood that the leap to a larger executive position was less about specific accomplishments and more about exhibiting leadership qualities that were recognized by the big bosses in her company.

She articulated to her boss at appropriate times (like her annual reviews) her desire for a bigger leadership role and asked for frank feedback on what she needed to work on to help her get there. Her prompting opened up a dialogue for coaching that helped her hone her leadership style in a way that remained quintessentially Kim but also helped her stay aware and manage her rough edges. She knew that she had a tendency to speak before fully collecting her thoughts, and also that she needed to think at an enterprise level, not always just about her own particular projects.

When the bigger role came up that she hoped would lead to an SVP title, which was to run customer service in social media, instead of just applying for the role and waiting for the interview process to start, Kim created a future vision presentation for how she saw customer service evolving through social media. She was passionate. Everyone dreads having to call customer service. She knew that her bank took nearly half a billion of these dreaded calls a year. She wanted to transform that experience and believed social media held the key. So she started talking about it that way. She wove this story in whenever she could in the context of her current job. And she asked to deliver her presentation of the future of customer service to her boss's boss.

This may seem like a bold move, but she made it clear that she wanted to serve the company. She confidently and passionately talked about value creation and expressed gratitude for all the opportunities she'd had at the company. While her presentation was well received, she did not get promoted.

Instead, a big reorganization happened, and Kim lost half her team and was layered under another manager. Instead of moving up, she felt as though she had been moved back. She could have quit during that time. She could have been pissed and dialed back her excellence. She could have whined to coworkers, poisoning the well at work with negativity. She did none of those things. Instead, she focused on supporting the goals of her new manager. She worked on raising the bar for her smaller team.

She focused on learning more in her desired area of growth. She identified people in her network who ran large customer service teams—something she had no experience with—and peppered them with questions so she could learn more. She discovered the "bible" on customer service operations and made it her bedtime reading. She attended a conference on customer service and talked to everyone she could.

Instead of being demoralized by her setback, she used it as a chance to raise her knowledge and skills while demonstrating that she was the kind of leader the company could count on to stay focused and positive during organizational upheavals—which is just part of life in a big enterprise.

Finally she landed the job, but it did not automatically come with the SVP title she craved. In truth, the new job was a lot more work and responsibility, without a commensurate pay increase. Gone were her easier, more "balanced" days. Now she was getting up at 5:30 AM to stay on top of all she was doing. There was a lot to build—it turned out that this team lacked all kinds of processes and functions. Kim had never worked harder in her life.

However, she did not expect to get paid more for not doing more, and she stayed patient, waiting for her upcoming salary review.

At her midyear review she was raised to the next pay level. At the end of the year she got the SVP title. The path may have been windier than she'd first hoped, and it required patience and persistence, but she got there. Her reward? She has settled into her brand-new role with grace—and in fact, despite the longer hours and more challenging problems, she has never been more energized to go to work. Still, she finds plenty of time to oversee the construction and pick out tiles. Her proud family will be moving into their completely remodeled home by summer.

don't wait for an invitation

Are you thinking about how to get ahead at the office? Here's a tip: don't wait for an invitation to add more value. Just go do it. Instead of focusing on titles and raises and politics and asking what your company has done for you lately, focus on identifying a problem that you could solve by bringing your talents to bear. What is the mission of the company, and how are you best using your gifts to deliver on it? What is the company's top strategic priority, and how can you develop yourself and others to make greater progress toward that goal? I am not telling you to *not* advocate for yourself by putting yourself up for promotion and actively discussing that with your leadership. I'm telling you to have the mind-set that will make your boss want to say yes.

do more, think less

Too often, people spend time thinking about what they should do long past the point of identifying the necessary action. This is procrastination, not planning or preparing. There's absolutely a place and time to obsess about the details. But be careful to stop your planning short of indulging in endless hemming and hawing and perfecting the unimportant. Avoid analysis paralysis. You can waste a ton of time doing things that aren't bringing you any closer to success.

I find that people often procrastinate or keep spinning their wheels on superfluous tasks out of fear—a fear of moving forward into the unknown. People get stymied by fear of failure or rejection and by stranger danger. Be honest with yourself about what's really going on if you are thinking too long and embrace the idea that forward momentum is essential.

If you've done a reasonable amount of homework, it's time for action. No matter where you want to go, getting there requires taking steps! Is there ever a perfect time to ask for a promotion, seek new clients, launch a product, go back to school, travel the world, change careers, have a baby, get back in shape, or start a new business? There is no such thing as the perfect time for anything in life. Doing something extraordinary is unlikely to be convenient, neatly scheduled for 10:00 AM on Tuesday, when you have no conflict around other work or leisure activities.

When we launched the precursor to WeddingChannel.com, I was amazed by the number of people who came up to me and said, "Wow, I had that idea!" or, "I was going to do that!" Jenny and I found this comical. Who *didn't* have the idea to put gift registries online? Here's the thing. We didn't just have the idea to do it. We did it.

It wasn't the perfect time—we had to drop out of business school to do it. It wasn't the most obvious decision, and we weren't 100 percent guaranteed to have a positive outcome. After all, we were first-time entrepreneurs who may have had experience in tech start-ups but literally knew nothing about the wedding or retail industry.

Less thinking,
more doing.

That's why I loved this line from the movie *The Social Network*: "If you had started Facebook," Mark Zuckerberg says, "you would have started Facebook." The doing is the difference.

Great ideas are worthless without action. Imperfect, consistent, glorious action.

Those who go on to create extraordinary things always start before others would deem them ready. They do the things others say they can't. They stick with them longer than others would. That's why confidence comes before competence, not the other way around. You don't have to be perfect to start, you have to start to be perfect.

Better to hop on the 80 percent right train and get somewhere than stand alone at the station waiting for the perfection train to come along. It's not coming. It must have gotten into a crash with the *Polar Express*.

pace yourself

You and only you decide your pace on your journey to extraordinary. At different times in your life, you may want to take it slower, or dial it up. If you enjoy a different pace, go for it. Factor that in. But don't expect to get to the same place as quickly as those going faster. They probably aren't enjoying the same views and experiences along the way as you are. Neither fast nor slow is better, they're just different. Embrace your *choice* and continue on your course.

Imagine you're a movie star who needs to get into shape for a new movie in which you play a superhero. How are you going to get ready for your HD beach scene in which you slay villains in your superhero bikini outfit? Filming starts in about three months, and you've got to get cracking if you're going to take off those twenty pounds. The studio hires you a fabulous celebrity trainer for twice-daily workouts. You devote four grueling hours a day to learning mixed martial arts and turning yourself into a lean, mean fighting machine. Additionally, you hire a personal chef, who puts you on a strict diet of steamed kale and quinoa. This aggressive pace comes with lots of trade-offs, but it will get you to where you need to be.

Let's consider another person who's also looking to shape up, but at a different pace. She's made a commitment to walk thirty minutes a day, every day, no matter what. And from now on, no more 3:00 PM strolls by the candy bowl in Accounting for a little afternoon pick-me-up. This plan and pace might result in moderate weight loss over time, and she will certainly be healthier, but she's not going to have ripped abs in three months. And that's okay. As long as she is not mismatching her expectations with insufficient action, she can be thrilled with her outcome. However, if you pine for the results that only come with a pace you are not eager to pursue, you will only feel dissatisfied.

Which pace would you choose? Personally, I'd rather live a life that includes an occasional cookie than have screen-ready abs. The point is, whatever goal you're striving for, don't pick a pace that will make you miserable. And don't expect the results of one pace when you are embracing another. Pick what you pick, and be happy with it.

make plan b part of your plan a

Now that we know that the road to extraordinary isn't just a path but rather an obstacle course, let's look ahead to see what we might need to leap over the hurdles. I call this making plan B part of my plan A. There are so many things that can crop up and thwart our best-laid plans. The weather. A traveling husband. A customer cancellation. A kid with an ear infection. The holidays. But none of these snafus have to be reasons why you don't show up for yourself.

You may not have planned on these bumps in the road, but they are not really out of the ordinary events, are they? If you want to make your goal a priority, anticipate what could trip you up. Go ahead and brainstorm every Armageddon-type disaster scenario that could throw you off. Now plan around it. How will you leap over those obstacles instead of ending up facedown on the ground eating dirt?

Your rent doesn't magically get lowered just because it snowed and a customer canceled. And, a plan B is not just for when you are in dire straits.

Take the example of a salesperson who has set her sights on earning the luxurious trip all the top performers are rewarded. To reach her goal, she needs $5,000 more in sales this month. Which of the following plans do you think is going to put her beachside, basking in the sun with rum punch in hand?

PLAN A: Aim for the minimum sales required and try to bring in those sales on the last day of the month.

PLAN B: Devote extra time early in the month to prospect for customers, setting up twice the required meetings. Create extra time to focus on earning this reward by planning for additional help, like a few more babysitting swap hours with a neighbor. Wake up thirty minutes earlier every day, and get work done before your sick child wakes up.

Now that example is very specific to someone in sales, but the point is this: Have you ever not gotten what you wanted because something derailed you from reaching your goal? In hindsight, could you have predicted that obstacle? If you had thought about it in advance, could you have come up with a plan B? Would anticipating the possibility of this snafu have made you feel calm and in control, versus frustrated and deflated?

Planning to do the minimum is not the way to maximize your joy in life. Recall the most influential mentor you've ever had in your life. Or bring to mind someone very accomplished whom you admire. Can you imagine this person ever advising you to just squeak by? To come in at the last minute and aim for the minimum? Doing that is not only ineffective but stressful—and very ordinary.

You can directly apply this plan B approach to any goal in your life, whether it's learning a drum solo, exercising more, adding amazing adventure and rewards to your life, or getting ahead at work. When you aim higher, when you anticipate and plan ahead, you are far better equipped to handle the obstacles that will inevitably arise.

reward yourself!

Do you want more rewards in your life? Decide to be self-motivated. Don't wait for someone else to set a bold goal and incentive plan for you. What are you waiting for? Work backward from your personal why and create your personal rewards plan.

Let me tell you about a woman, Wendy, who was able to overcome obstacles and achieve extraordinary goals by rewarding herself along the way. After years of doing odd jobs, with her lemon of an ex-husband's voice telling her she wasn't good at anything, Wendy signed up to be a Stylist with Stella & Dot. In 2014 she stood up at a team meeting and announced that she was going to do 100 trunk shows by the end of the year. As with any bold goal, she encountered some naysayers, who thought she was actually joking. But Wendy is the type of person who says, "Don't believe me—just watch." Now she was more motivated than ever. Boldly sharing her plan with her three kids, she set four goals, all with matching rewards:

1. When she hit twenty-five trunk shows, they'd go to Great Wolfe Lodge for a weekend.

2. When she hit fifty trunk shows, they'd take an awesome camping trip.

3. When she hit seventy-five trunk shows, they'd take a dream trip to Disneyland.

4. When she reached 100 trunk shows, she'd make a down payment on a house!

In the first couple of months, she was able to book forty trunk shows. Then things came to a screeching halt. It was summer, and no one was around. People canceled. "Of course, I started to doubt myself, but then I'd look at my goals on the wall and into the eyes of my children and I'd keep going. I just had to work harder and smarter," she remembers. No doubt, laying out rewards along the way not only motivated her but garnered plenty of encouragement from her children!

Luckily, Wendy has an amazing mother who was willing to watch her kids when she did some of those trunk shows. Along the way, the Baby Daddy came in and out, causing disruption, pain, and distraction. Her three-year-old twin girls got the normal colds that toddlers get in winter. Yet Wendy kept plugging away. After all, she had a powerful *why* as well as more rewards to unlock for herself and her three children.

By the end of the year, Wendy had surpassed her goal, with a total of III trunk shows. She made a down payment on a family house, and she was featured in *Redbook* magazine. For her, the looks of pride on her children's faces when they saw their mommy featured in a magazine was the best and most unexpected reward of all. "I never could imagine the outcome of all my hard work—my entire life has changed. I've learned something so important: how hard work, clear goals, and the willingness to stick to it is life-altering! It's impacted all of us—even my seven-year-old son going into second grade has set a goal to read one hundred chapter books this year—he's already at number forty-two!" Turns out, our children don't need to be an excuse why we can't accomplish something—instead, they can be a reason why we must.

Wendy had more obstacles in her path than most people typically experience, and she succeeded anyway. She had plenty of reasonable excuses that might have kept her from accomplishing such wild, high-bar goals, but she kept showing up for herself, no matter what.

Why wait to stretch yourself until someone else sets a challenge or dangles a carrot in front of you? When you learn how to break down your own goals into a fun series of challenges, you've made it ten times easier to achieve the extraordinary.

how to pivot: don't stay wrong for long

Pivot could be one of the most overused buzzwords in Silicon Valley. There is good reason for that, though. It's what you do when you are banging your head against the wall because your path has led to a dead end.

I want you to visualize a ball-in-a-maze puzzle. The ball has to be navigated past a series of holes and obstacles to get to the winning part of the labyrinth. You tip the puzzle to get the ball down a path, but it ends up in a dead end. What do you do? Should you shake the puzzle super-hard so that the ball slams even more into the wooden dead end? Or should you stop, reassess, back up a bit, and gently navigate the ball down a different, probably better path?

Hitting a dead end *does not* mean there is no solution to the puzzle. The goal of completing the puzzle does not need to change. Your approach does, though. You've heard it said a million times: the definition of insanity is repeating the same experiment and expecting different results.

Don't be wrong for long. Just back up, learn from your mistakes, and then pivot.

There will be times on your journey to extraordinary when you'll need to change your approach. Sometimes your mistakes will be painful. Well, if you are going through hell, just keep going. Sometimes the only way out is through. I have made many a midcourse correction, both in my personal and professional life.

Here's one example. Our goal in building the Stella & Dot Family of Brands has always been to offer the definitive, the best, and the most flexible business opportunity possible. We back up this goal with the best product, the best technology, the best service, the best training, and the very best compensation plan suited for the modern way people want to work. With our high sales averages, our dollars per hour is an outlier in the industry. For a retail seller, which the vast majority of independent business owners are, we have always been hands-down the best. In 2014, however, we realized that we weren't offering the best we could offer to those who were taking on leadership roles within our company and helping to train and coach the other business owners. When we launched, only 60 percent of our force had other full- or part-time jobs outside the home; now its 80 percent. Our original compensation plan was not optimized for that.

For the first time in our short history, our growth was slowing, and thus our impact. Our field leaders, who previously had experienced only strong and continued growth, were trying to figure out reasonable expectations for themselves and their teams. We knew we were nowhere near our market share potential. Accessories are a $30 billion industry, and we had barely scratched it.

It was time for a change. We did deep analysis, and then we overhauled our compensation plan. We made a decision that served the mission and created the most opportunity for all. It was expensive and challenging to take out the sledgehammer and build a new plan from scratch. From start to finish, we went through 18 months of running analytics, gathering feedback from our field, implementing tests, reanalyzing, fine-tuning, training, and evolving.

The result: our core North American business is again experiencing tremendous growth. But we had to hit a few dead ends in order to get through to even more extraordinary.

You may have the same experience in life. You want to change careers, so you need to take a lower-paying position just to get a foot in a new door. You have to go back to school to switch to an entirely new career. It may be a tough transition, but if making it will get you to more opportunity, to something you are passionate about, it's worth it.

heard on the path to ordinary

I am just so crazy busy!

That may work for that person, but I'm not _____.

It's not fair.

I have been thinking about that a ton . . .

I have really been meaning to do that . . .

No. That is not going to work.

But I already tried that.

That's just my problem. It's my personality . . .

heard on the path to extraordinary

What I like about that idea is . . .

Let's just get going and we'll figure it out!

Let's focus. Is this important to the outcome a year from now?

Well, we've survived worse!

This may not come natural to me, but what the heck, it's not going to kill me!

Okay, creative people, what's the work-around?

This is a minor setback. Not exactly life-or-death.

To make your way toward success on the path of least regret, remember to:

- Focus on creating value to move along your path. Never bring a sense of entitlement with you.
- See setbacks as bumps in the right road, not a sign that says DEAD END. Abandoning the trail won't get you there faster, it will just get you lost.
- Be patient. Opportunity doesn't come knocking on your schedule. Good things come to those who persist.
- It's not life-or-death. Taking yourself too seriously sucks up the energy you need to be awesome. Lighten up and get going. If you don't go the right way immediately, so what? Just dust yourself off, find the humor, and give it another go.
- Don't go it alone. Whether it's the support of a business partner, a friend, or a spouse, sharing your goals and finding someone to keep you accountable will help you stay the course. Look for straight shooters who will be loving, but won't just listen to you moan and groan. Moaning and groaning doesn't pay the mortgage.
- Don't think about what is possible for the person you used to be last year. Instead, think about what is possible for the person you want to become.
- Effort is 100 percent choice.

CHAPTER 5

the power of a positive mind

Lively up yourself, don't be no drag.
—BOB MARLEY

Success is walking from failure to failure with no loss of enthusiasm.
—WINSTON CHURCHILL

S OMETIMES I'M SO POSITIVE I ANNOY MYSELF. IT'S true, *we all* have a side that finds ranting a relief and seeks commiseration. But I'm going to convince you that learning how to shift into your positive mind will help you accomplish what you want with far *less* effort. Being positive is simply more effective and efficient. There's nothing negative about being positive and nothing positive about being negative.

First, let's clear up some misunderstandings and inaccurate associations. Being optimistic does not require being an idiot. This is not about burying your head in the sand so you don't have to see or acknowledge problems. It's not about spinning your story or situation toward the positive to look better to others.

Having a positive mind-set means that you see where you are, and if you don't like it, you simply move on to look for a better way forward.

Nothing
is more powerful
than a
positive mind.

Did you see the movie *Inside Out*? If not, run, don't walk. It's a fantastic way to wrap your beautiful mind around the concept of developing a positive mind. We all have different emotions that live in our heads—some positive, some negative, some protective. In *Inside Out* we travel inside the head of the main character, a young girl named Riley. In her head, her emotions turn into animated characters with names like Joy, Disgust, Sadness, Anger, and Fear. These characters (i.e., her emotions) man the control panels of her thoughts, and her thoughts determine how she reacts to the world around her. (Dear Disney, this Pixar movie will be accepted as only a partial apology for so many films where you kill off the mom and then send a girl to find a man to solve all of her problems.)

This movie playfully shows how powerful our emotions are, how our minds work, and how we can learn to control our thoughts. It's a powerful message—and one not just for kids. I have studied the Enneagram, analyzed Carol Dweck's research on growth and fixed mind-sets, and read tons of other books and articles by other positive psychology experts. I've come to believe that the work I do on my mind-set is far more impactful, and has had much more tangible, successful results, than the business books or tech-focused papers I read to stay up to date.

When I first started learning about positive psychology and mindfulness, I was skeptical. I feared it would all be a bunch of touchy-feely mumbo-jumbo. Yet when I dug in and came to understand the neuroscience behind it, I was convinced that focusing on taking control of my brain would make not only me happier; it would make the people I love and share my life with happier, too.

During most of the 20th century, most neuroscientists believed that the brain structure is relatively fixed after early childhood. More recent findings reveal that the brain actually remains plastic into adulthood, which means that we can change our mind-set, our thoughts, and even our habits with mental exercises. Sorry, no more excuses that sound like "I can't help it—that's just the way I'm wired!" If the way you think does not serve you, change the way you think.

In my own quest for self-improvement, I joined a group called the Young Presidents Organization (YPO), which focuses on the personal development of executives under the age of fifty. It was through this group that I first met Shirzad Chamine, author of the *New York Times* bestseller *Positive Intelligence* (Greenleaf, 2012). In his book, Shirzad pulls together decades of research from neuroscience and motivational theories to show people how to shift their negative thinking into empowering ways of thinking, acting, and feeling. After being convinced that Shirzad was the real deal, and that his approach and techniques really worked, I invited him to speak to our top field leaders at a directors' retreat and to spend two days with our Stella & Dot executive team in Half Moon Bay, California. We went through a lot of life-changing work together that weekend—work that has transformed how I think and how I lead our company.

The gist of positive psychology is this: the more you train your brain to be positive, the happier you feel. The more you calm your mind and focus on being positive, the more synapses and neurons your brain will create that support a calm and positive thought process.

Just as you need a healthy habit of exercise to have a strong body, you need a healthy habit of mental exercise to create a fit mind. This mental exercise will literally change your brain's structure and capabilities. Yes, you can rewire your brain to be less afraid, to believe your dreams can come true, and to believe that your efforts will make an impact.

I like to think of mental exercises as outlook shifters. While you may never evict Negative Nelly from your head, you can certainly exile her to a tiny bedroom in the basement of your brain with no electricity or air-conditioning.

I have felt such a powerful personal transformation that I have become a huge advocate of mindfulness and try to share it with as many people as I can. Most important, I'll tell you how I've created a quick and effective practice of mindfulness that you can easily integrate into your life today.

your thoughts are not you, and they are not all true

According to the Laboratory of Neuro Imaging at the University of Southern California, we humans have anywhere from 12,000 to 60,000 thoughts per day, and as many as 98 percent of them are exactly the same thoughts we had the day before. Talk about creatures of habit! Even more significant, 80 percent of our thoughts are negative. Sounds depressing, right? Are we just wired to worry?

You will never find an off button for all of your negative thoughts. And that's okay. Recognize that such thoughts are part of our evolutionary heritage. *You are normal.* Don't beat yourself up for having a tendency to beat yourself up, and remember that you're not the only one. We all do it, and there is a very logical reason why we evolved this way. Our negative thoughts are linked to the healthy paranoia we needed to survive in our cave-dwelling past.

This doesn't mean, however, that you can't change.

Shirzad personifies our negative voices into 10 distinct mental saboteurs with names like Judge, Controller, Stickler, Victim, and

Avoider. When unchecked, these voices can wreak havoc with your life. When you become self-aware, however, you can shift from self-sabotage to optimal performance using simple and proven neuroscience-based techniques.

First, ask yourself if you believe that all of your thoughts are true. Spoiler alert: they are not. That is why there is always a difference between what people say, what people mean, and what people hear. Our thoughts are not facts.

When you think of the ticker tape of thoughts in your brain in this way, you can see why it's critical to step back and consider your thoughts carefully. Start with:

The story I am telling myself is _____, but
- Is this thought true?
- Is this thought important?
- Is this thought helpful?

Be wary of thoughts that read as overly dramatic, seductive, cruel, paranoid, or self-aggrandizing. These thoughts might sound understanding, or even flattering, but if you don't question them you risk moving in the opposite direction of your goals.

Let's go back to a physical example we can all relate to. You go into a store dressing room before a beach vacation. Looking in the mirror, you ignore your gorgeous eyes and smile and zoom in on the spot on your body you don't like. Forget the fact that it's awesome that you have two working legs. You have cruel, dramatic thoughts like, *Ugh, I hate my thighs.* Pretty soon, things turn ugly. *I'm disgusting! I need to go on a cleanse.* Moments earlier, you caught yourself in the reflection of a mirror and you were looking good. How could you have changed so drastically? You didn't. You shifted into a negative mind-set and your spin factory began work-ing overtime. It's time to shift positive.

Actively noticing when your thoughts seem overly dramatic can clue you in to thoughts that are just that—thoughts, not facts.

You also have to separate your thoughts from who you are as a person. Even if a cruel thought comes up, about yourself or someone else, you can rephrase it in your mind to be a heck of a lot closer to the truth. For example, are you berating yourself for doing something stupid? Instead of saying, *I'm a loser,* say, *I'm hav-ing the thought that I'm a loser.* The difference is subtle, but it can help you understand that *you* are not your thoughts. Just like you are not the results of your every action. Next, try, *My actions didn't work out this time, but that is not a reflection of who I am as a person and what I am capable of.*

What about when your inner Victim takes control? When you find yourself thinking something like: *How could she have done that to me?* This is the perfect time to take a reality check. Try, *The story I am telling myself is, when she said this, she was trying to hurt me. Alternatively . . .*

Thinking like a victim is a common and powerful saboteur to happiness. It's normal to slip into this mind-set, which is why it's critical that you learn to recognize it and promptly slip back out of it.

say thanks but no thanks to your mind

When you find yourself overthinking and you notice that your thoughts have turned negative, just say no. Cautious thoughts are there to help protect you, but you can choose whether you pay attention to them or not.

Many times our thoughts involve the same old stories, like, *I don't really know what I'm doing.* One of our favorite head lies is that we are incompetent and others are about to call us out on it at any moment. When you hear yourself chatting away about self-doubt, stamp it out. *Oh, here's the ole "I'm incompetent" story that everyone tells themselves.*

Let's take the story of a brave, smart, and capable woman who chose to return to work after an eight-year gap raising kids. The family had managed to live comfortably on her husband's salary, but when they decided to send their kids to private school, they knew that would require two incomes.

She had worked *a lot* during her time as a stay-at-home mom, but not at something she felt looked good on a résumé. Had she stayed at her "real job," she'd have been a vice president by this time. But she had left off at senior manager and now felt totally out of date on her industry. Her positive mind knew that she was so happy she made the choices she did. She had loved being a stay-at-home mom and wouldn't have traded that experience for the world.

Her goal was to look for a job in the fall when the kids started school. But when the time came, her negative mind told her no one was going to want to hire her. She would certainly be undervalued. It wasn't fair. Even though their higher expenses had started, her job hunting had not, which started to cause tension in her marriage because she had been the one who insisted on private school. And, she said she was eager to go back to work. She was always *thinking* about going back to work, but she never actually did something about it.

Then, a month later, she had a wake-up moment when giving advice to her own child, who was settling into his new school.

"Middle school is a big change from elementary—so it may take a few months before you feel at home. If you want to make friends, you are just going to have to go over there and ask to join in on the game. I know you miss your old friends, but honey, it's time for you to move forward. It's just how life goes! The more you try, the faster you will grow to love it! You'll figure it out!" She suddenly realized she was telling her kid to be brave, but she was modeling fear in her life. She had to follow her own advice.

With a positive mind, she dusted off the cobwebs and started networking with friends. She kept reminding herself that she had to take the initiative to ask others to join the game! Within a couple of months, she landed a four-day-a-week job that worked for her hybrid working-mom life.

The point is that your negative thoughts do not have to guide your actions—or cause inaction. If your negative thoughts are telling you that you can't do something, prove them wrong by going out there and doing it. After all, it's hard to undermine your goals when you're actively pursuing them.

what's going on in your mind?

Which voices are the loudest in your head? To find out, take the Saboteur Assessment, a free five-minute quiz at Shirzad Chamine's website (www.PositiveIntelligence.com). For links to more free assessment resources go to www.helloextraordinary .com.

Isn't it shocking how well an Internet quiz has you pegged? See, you are not such a mystery and in fact are pretty normal. Understanding your personality will help you be more aware of the types of negative voices that tend to crop up in your unique head. Then, when you recognize them, you can kick them to the curb.

give your brain a break

Do you feel frenzied on a daily basis? Are you a slave to your smartphone, constantly getting a hit of your data crack by checking email, Instagram, and Twitter in every spare second?

Do you check email while going to the bathroom or, even worse, while driving? When you sit on the coach watching TV, are you also checking Facebook on your iPad? Do you feel stressed out, tired, and overwhelmed most days? Getting a handle on your multitasking lifestyle can make a tremendous difference to your ability to create and live in a positive mind-set.

If you're a working parent like me, your home environment is probably filled with love, but a bit chaotic. You're in a state of constant stimulation—responding to requests from little people, changing diapers, or figuring out the week's pickup/drop-off requirements, all over a din of bizarre YouTube clips in the background. No wonder so many people feel like they have a burned-out brain.

All this information overload is an enemy of positivity. A stressed-out brain creates a negative mind. Your brain needs a break—the mental equivalent of a holiday in Hawaii. It's when you feel like you don't have any time for yourself that you need it the most. You cannot be extraordinary if you are grumpy, frazzled, and tired.

So what exactly gives your brain a break? Call it mindfulness, call it meditation, or call it quieting your mind. Whatever you call it, it works and will make you a less stressed, less tired, less negative person who has the energy and excitement to be extraordinary. And the good news is that it's a lot easier and a lot less boring than you think.

If you had asked me about meditation five years ago, I would have scoffed. For me, meditation conjured up an image of trying to sit still, cross-legged, in a room full of burning incense and Tibetan monks. Other guests would be there dressed in hemp clothing, looking earthy and smelling unshowered. About thirty seconds in, I would be bored out of my mind, wondering when I could get up. I'd be in mental anguish with thoughts like: *I'm hungry. I have to go to the bathroom. My neck hurts. I hate monks.* Minutes would feel like hours, and then flies would land on my face and I would be so disturbed I would frantically swat them away. The monks would give me the stink-eye and kick me out. I would fail terribly at meditation. Meditation, I felt certain, was not for me.

In case you too have creatively negative interpretations of what is actually required to be mindful, let me reframe it for you: being mindful is just chilling a bit during the day to give your brain a break. Monks and incense are *not* required. Let me lay out all the benefits so you are motivated to meditate.

Giving your brain a break offers you these proven benefits:

- It lowers stress. Research published in the journal *Health Psychology* shows that mindfulness is associated with feeling less stressed because it actually lowers levels of the stress hormone cortisol.
- Research published in *Frontiers in Human Neuroscience* shows that the benefits linger. Even when you get busy again, your brain is still benefiting, much like your metabolism after you stop exercising. Why? Because your brain's neural connections settle down with meditation. You release more dopamine, the "happy" neurotransmitter. Your brain and your body simply calm down.
- Meditation also makes you nicer because you are less

moody and you sleep better. Do you want to be in better control of your moods? Isn't that easier when you are rested?

- Meditation benefits the people you interact with, by making you more compassionate. Yes, you will in fact yell at your kids a lot less, and you will not assume that the woman who accidentally bumped into you at the grocery store is the incarnation of evil.

Okay, if you are not yet convinced, let me throw in this bonus benefit. Meditation supports weight loss. Trying to drop a few pounds? According to a survey of psychologists conducted by *Consumer Reports* and the American Psychological Association, mindfulness training was considered an "excellent" or "good" strategy for weight loss by seven out of ten psychologists. How's that for positive results?

When you shift into your positive mind through simple meditation, you will find that you feel *and* express:

- Curiosity instead of anger
- Appreciation instead of frustration
- Trust instead of distrust
- Willingness instead of resistance
- Hope instead of doom

And what if, to get these benefits, all you have to do is spend fifteen minutes a day relaxing your brain, in easy five-minute increments? Give it a week, and I can promise that you will be a happier, more positive, and more productive person by the end of it. You'll have negative thoughts still, of course, but they'll be quieter, they'll come less frequently, and you'll recover—shifting back to positive—far more quickly. The good news is that you will feel the benefits of meditation right away, so you'll be motivated to stick with it.

And the people around you will benefit too, as your positivity rubs off on them. You'll feel appreciated and surrounded by loving, competent people. You'll also think they are much less annoying. It's amazing how much better everyone else gets when you work on yourself.

mini mental vacays— three times a day

I take three mini mental vacays every day, by habit, so I can regularly recharge my mind. When I first tried this, I thought I couldn't possibly make time to stick with it. But is fifteen minutes a day really too much to ask to have peace of mind? I just had to figure out how to make that fifteen minutes easily fit into the 1,440 minutes we all have each day. When I thought of it that way, I realized that spending 1 percent of my time relaxing my mind so I could improve the other 99 percent of my life seemed like a good deal.

I tried it, and I was stunned at the results. I really did feel better almost instantly. I was less tired physically. I was present more of the time and more productive and efficient at work. I was calmer and more at ease. And yes—I was happier!

I highly recommend that you read *Positive Intelligence* to gain a better understanding if you are interested. That said, the book recommends you count your meditation with a point system that adds up to 100 each day. That just wasn't something I was sticking to, so I had to find my own, simpler habit of meditation. I found that if something was hard, I needed to find a way to make it easy

It's amazing
how much better
everyone else gets
when you work
on yourself.

so that I could stick to it. That's why I came up with the concept of three mini mental vacays a day. To help me not forget, I attach each mental break to an existing ritual: my morning coffee or morning run, lunch, my drive home from work, or right before I go to sleep.

My mini mental vacay is simply a five-minute period when I quiet my mind, let go of busy chatter, and give my brain a break so that I can recharge my batteries. It's as simple as deciding to relax and do nothing while I have that cup of coffee versus checking my email. Here's how you do it.

Become more present in your physical body and take in the world around you, becoming aware of how each part of you feels, and

SEE your physical environment.
TOUCH texture and take notice of how your body feels.
SMELL the fresh air and scents around you.
HEAR the sounds around you.
TASTE your food or drink.
RELEASE other interrupting thoughts.
REFLECT on thoughts, feelings, and events that make you
     happy and that you feel grateful for.

Don't overthink this exercise. I zoom in on one sense for about a minute, and then move on to the next. Sometimes, especially when I am in a very beautiful place taking in nature, I focus mostly on sight and sound. I naturally drift toward gratitude and that always goes right to the faces of my family. I reflect on a person, song, place, or thing that fills me with a sense of love and gratitude.

Don't freak out if your brain is not 100 percent Zen master. Random thoughts will try to steal your attention. *What time is that meeting? I can't believe she sent me that email!* Just RELEASE these thoughts. Imagine yourself on the side of a country road, where those thoughts are like cars driving by. They come into your view, pass by, and then quickly zoom away. Let them. Don't run into traffic, and certainly don't chase after them. Just let them go.

wake up on the right side of your head

What's the first thing you do when you wake up? Do you grab your phone and check your inbox or your latest social media addiction? Swap out this busy brain ritual. Instead, starting your day with a peaceful mind can make all the difference in your day. Check your body and your gratitude instead of your inbox.

Here are a few more rituals that can help you throughout the day:

- SAY HELLO HAPPY: Always take a mini mental vacay (even if it's just one to two minutes) before interacting with a new group of people, especially the most important people—your family. Reflect first on what you love about these people. This will make you as excited to see them as your dog is to see you. A sixty-second, active reflection on what you love about the people you are about to see will do wonders for your ability to be truly present and will make the time much more enjoyable and meaningful for all.

- BEDTIME WIND-DOWN: Make your last ritual of the day one of calm, not clutter. Instead of spending more quality time with all your little screens, try stretching or meditating as the last thing you do before bed. The blue light is disturbing your sleep anyway. Feel like you are too rushed to do this? Wake up earlier, go to bed earlier. And let's be honest: are you really going to miss that extra five minutes of really bad reality TV or web browsing?

Which of these mini mental vacays can you commit to trying today?

focus on the opportunity, not the obstacles

Opportunity is all around you, but if you are too busy gawking at obstacles, you'll be blinded to those opportunities. Staring at an obstacle for a long time isn't resting or strategizing. It's just self-sabotage.

Obstacle finding is actually a part of most business school curricula. It's prudent to think ahead and identify the barriers you will face. But be sure you spend the right amount of time on opportunity finding. You can look at the 100 reasons why your endeavor won't work, but to be successful you need to stay focused on the reasons why it will.

Instead, I want you to imagine opportunity hanging from the chandelier, lounging in the chairs around you, and sitting cross-legged on the floor. It's truly everywhere, hanging out, just waiting for you to notice.

laugh it off

A little levity can go a long way. Humor is one of the best tools available to push yourself away from wallowing and into actually *doing* something to change a circumstance you don't like. I can go from being very, very angry to cracking myself up. Seeing the humor in a situation is just a trigger to say to myself, *Okay, the pointless pity party is now over. What am I going to do to change what I don't like?*

Brace yourself. This next mind-set shifter is going to sound ridiculous—because it *is* ridiculous. That's why it works.

Try taking your most common negative thought. What is it right now? It could be something like: *My boss just tore me down in that meeting. He is evil. He is out to get me!* Or: *I am not accomplishing as much as I should be. I am such a loser!* Maybe it's: *This was a total waste of time and money! I am an idiot!*

Now, in your head, sing that thought as if you were appearing onstage in a melodrama—the type of play in which everything is dramatically overdone. Even mentally dress yourself in a top hat or a wide hoop skirt. Singing your negative thoughts usually reveals right away that they're a bit overdramatic. Right? That's because they often *are*.

Being able to laugh at myself has always been my saving grace. Don't take your thoughts so seriously. Find the funny that ends your pity party.

don't look at what is, look at what could be

I met Juvenal Chavez and his three sons at the Ernst & Young Entrepreneur of the Year reception a few years ago. I was honored to be among the candidates for the award, but after meeting Juvenal and hearing his story, I wanted to run around the room shouting, "Vote for Juvenal!"

Juvenal came to the United States in 1984. He had been a high school teacher in Mexico who wanted a better life for his kids. So he moved to California at age twenty-five with his wife, Maria Elena, and his eldest son, Juvenal Jr. There he went to night school to learn English while the family supported themselves with various jobs— Maria Elena as a housekeeper, Juvenal as a janitor by day and a bartender at night. Then a friend offered him a job washing test tubes at a lab at Stanford for $14 an hour. To him this was a huge advancement—not only because he would be earning more money hourly but also because he'd be cleaning test tubes instead of toilets.

Around the same time his brother approached Juvenal about a business idea—opening a meat market. The idea immediately appealed to Juvenal because he saw a market as a way for families like theirs to stay connected to their ancestral homeland. His meat market would be much more than a store—it would be a place where Mexican Americans like him and his family could shop for familiar food in a familiar environment. So Juvenal took his wife to look at the property. They walked into the hole-in-the-wall and were immediately hit with the stench of rotten meat and saw flies everywhere.

He backed out of the small, cramped space in disgust, saying, "I cannot buy into this! What a horrible place! Maria Elena, let's go."

But Maria Elena stopped him in the parking lot and said, "Don't look at the shop as it is. Look at it through *your* eyes. Look at what it could be."

Juvenal listened. His wife's words rang true deep inside of him, and suddenly Juvenal saw the future in that moment. He looked again. He saw a bustling market, like the ones he missed from Mexico, right there. A market that was just right for the Bay Area's growing population of Latino families, who cooked for big groups, shopped more often, and ate different foods. He saw a friendly place, staffed by familiar faces who would help customers pick the ripest tomatillos for that night's dinner for twelve, while asking about their children.

From that vision more than twenty years ago, he and his three sons built an extraordinary grocery business, Mi Pueblo Food Center, which is now a $300 million Northern California grocery chain with twenty-one stores known for providing an authentic Latino shopping experience.

What if, in that critical moment in the meat market after his first reaction was one of disgust, he hadn't been with his positive wife, whose optimism and belief beyond reason shifted him into his positive mind? He would have never seen what could be—or had the guts to go create it.

If you want to make your life extraordinary, shift to your positive mind and then look again. Look for what others can't yet see.

Remember when my business partner Jenny and I were told we were naive? We were just thinking with a positive mind. Some of us are born with a glass-half-full mentality, and some of us aren't, but *all of us* have the ability to shift into a positive mind-set.

ask what good can come from something bad

Now I know what you are thinking. When you are feeling down, disappointed, frustrated, and "less than," and somebody says to you, "Maybe some good will come of this," it's irritating. No question. When something bad happens, who is really in the mood to focus on the good? Yet shifting your mind-set this way is incredibly powerful.

Good can come from even tragic events. Every one of the partners the Stella & Dot Foundation supports was started by a mother who faced a great personal difficulty. Out of their own dire circumstances, they found the strength and inspiration to help others. Christy Turlington Burns nearly died while giving birth to her first child. This harrowing experience led her to start Every Mother Counts, a foundation that supports maternal health all over the world. She is working to change the fact that a woman dies of childbirth-related causes every two minutes somewhere in the world.

Noreen Frazer has lived with stage 4 breast cancer for more than ten years. She got busy doing good because she believes that cancer can be something we can live with instead of die from. She realizes that a cure may not be found in her lifetime, but she has daughters she can fight for.

Holly Robinson Peete is doing the same thing through Holly-Rod, the foundation that she runs with her husband, former NFL pro football player Rodney Peete. They first launched the foundation in support of Parkinson's disease research and treatment programs. Then their eldest son, RJ, was diagnosed with autism. Rather than solely focusing on the struggles they had ahead of them, they realized that they had an opportunity to expand the foundation's mission to include raising money for autism research.

All of these women understand the power of positivity and of giving back despite one's own struggles. It's inspiring for sure. But do you think finding the good in a bad situation is only possible for celebrities with foundations? And is this only to be done when health is at risk? No, it's not. Finding the gift in a bad situation is an active choice you can make in your daily life.

Every time you encounter a bad situation, instead of focusing on how much it sucks, imagine at least one scenario in which something positive comes from it. It doesn't matter how small or trivial that gift is—it's about taking control of your thoughts and shifting your outlook to the positive. Doing this with the small things in life will increase your ability to do this under more dire situations.

Imagine you put your foot in your mouth, saying something that embarrasses you and offends others in a meeting or social situation. How can any good come from this? 1) If you step up to apologize, this could garner the respect of the other party and improve your future relationship. 2) This embarrassment guides you to pause before you speak, allowing you to get more out of conversations with others.

Just the act of this positive brainstorm will interrupt you berating yourself.

"comparison is the thief of joy"

It was Theodore Roosevelt who had the insight: "Comparison is the thief of joy." He was right. Comparison does steal joy—and it can also rob you of your self-confidence, if you let it.

I was once invited to speak on a panel at *Fortune*'s "The Most Powerful Women" conference, moderated by Rosie O'Donnell and featuring other entrepreneurs, including Tyra Banks, the supermodel-turned-businesswoman. Since my dad lived nearby, I asked him to join me. It was a proud father moment, for sure, as my dad watched from the audience.

After the panel discussion, the participants filed offstage and *Fortune* had a photographer waiting to snap our photos. My dad rushed over to me while I waited in the line. You need to know, Larry is very hard of hearing. "You were excellent! Now, of course, I couldn't hear a word you were saying! But I could just tell you were great!" The crowd could have been throwing rotten tomatoes at me—and he would still have thought I was fantastic. Who knows if I was actually great, but feeling unconditional love makes everyone *feel* great.

Then it was my turn to get my picture taken. I smiled for the camera. The photographer kept looking into the screen on the back of his camera and shaking his head, like he was trying to shake off a bad pitch.

Finally, in exasperation, he said to me, "No, not like that, pose like this!" He turned his camera around and showed me the pictures he had taken of the person right before me—Tyra Banks. He flipped our photos back and forth, saying, "See, this is you. This is Tyra. This is you, this is Tyra."

I looked at the pictures and instantly went from cloud nine to hideous trolldom. No regular woman should be put into an A/B eye exam flip test with a supermodel.

But then my mind went back to my father and what he saw in me that day when he was looking up at me from the audience. I was great! I just started laughing and put my hand on the photographer's shoulder and said, "Sir, get a hold of yourself! That woman is a supermodel. The pictures of me are what they are." But no wonder I began making plans to start a skincare line after that!

Joking aside, compared to the supermodel, I was horrendous. But when I saw myself through the eyes of my father, I felt great about myself.

Yes, there are people who have more and better—better education, connections, experience, beauty, brains, height, weight, talent. But there are also multitudes of people who have less and still are successful and happy. Be inspired by the greatness in others, but don't let noticing it lessen your appreciation for what you have or make you feel less.

assume the world is awaiting your success

People talk about how difficult it is for women to raise venture capital in Silicon Valley because it's a boys' club. When I went to raise money for my first start-up, I just put that out of my head. It may be true that it was (and still is) largely a boys' club, but dwelling on that wasn't going to help me get cash in the bank. I didn't shrink back. After all, our success was not predicated on everyone being open-minded. We just needed one term sheet out of hundreds of potential investors. I walked into countless rooms of all men and pitched my business, ignoring my gender and assuming they were listening without bias. Actually, in my personal experience, venture capitalists tend to be much more interested in how much return a business will generate and the overall track record and talent of the team than in the color or gender of the founders.

My goal was simply to work with the best. In the end, not only did we get funded by one of the most prestigious firms in the Valley at the time, but I was backed by Doug Mackenzie, who has been one of my greatest mentors for twenty years. (Doug is also the first investor in Stella & Dot and serves on the board.)

What is the moral of this story? All along, I could have focused on the few people who made sexist comments, but I was too busy moving on to the next meeting to even think about them. At this point in my career, I could write an entire book on the inappropriate comments I've received because of my gender—from my first boss at Baskin-Robbins when I was fifteen to potential investors to male employees who have worked for me. But I think that would be a real waste of paper and time. In most cases, all that was required to deal with them was a steely look of disdain. Trust me, I didn't work with those people for long.

A well-known journalist who does extraordinary work shining the light on women's issues once told me that I should be angrier about the inequities that women still face in the world, and in particular about the gender leadership gap in Silicon Valley. My tendency to focus on progress and the positive is not an inability to see the full scope of the problem. Oh, I see the problems, all right. I just don't find anger to be an effective response for me. My approach is not the *only* way to give a voice to women's issues, but I believe it's an important one.

Does this mean sexist comments are okay? Of course not. I hope my daughters face far fewer of them. But you don't have to let them zap you of your confidence or your positivity. I like to assume the world is awaiting my success—and I think you should, too. My best advice to you is this: assume that your gender, your ethnicity, and your age are not issues. Go forward as if the world is awaiting your success.

positively extraordinary

- Accept that you can reshape your brain. Your negative thoughts are not who you are. You are who you want to be. #neuroplasticitybaby!
- Benefit from mental exercises that are key to your well-being. The more you do them, the easier and more natural they become.
- Ignore the haters. They will always be there, but you decide whether or not to let them drag you down.
- Embrace that you need to be positive to help the people around you thrive. You can choose to be the person who lifts others up, or the person who brings them down.
- Find the silver lining. If you can't see there is potential good in a situation, you can't make it happen.
- If you are going to spend any of your precious energy doubting something, doubt your limits, not your abilities.

people

One universe, 9 planets, 204
countries, 809 islands, 7 seas, and I
had the pleasure of meeting you.

S TELLA & DOT IS NOT MY SUCCESS STORY. I MIGHT
technically have started the company, but I didn't create
the movement that is Stella & Dot all alone. It is the sum
of the success of every person, past or present, who has ever played
a part, big or small, in our company. The hilarious YouTube video
"The Lone Nut" points out the importance of the role played by
each of the different people involved in building a true movement.
Founders are often over-glorified nut jobs, myself included. A
founder hasn't created much until she has followers—the brave
people whose involvement, passion, and willingness to believe in
the lone nut create the energy and the critical mass to make radical
change. That's how movements really begin.

These so-called followers are actually leaders too. Case in
point: I would simply be a lone nut if not for the support of some
other extraordinary people—Janice Parsons, Maya Brenner, Doug
Mackenzie, Mike Lohner, Danielle Redner, and Blythe Harris. Not
to mention every single member of our home office team, the sales
field, and every single customer we've ever had.

People—the way others make us feel, how we help one another
become our best selves, what we do for and with one another—

are what makes the world go round. What is worth having if you can't share it? People are the most important part of the equation when you are making your life extraordinary. If you are human, you need love and care to be happy. If you are not impacting people or being acknowledged by others, what's the point?

The people we surround ourselves with can either help us or hinder us on our journey. But when we consciously choose to surround ourselves with positive people who lift us up, instead of dragging us down, we triple our chances for creating extraordinary in our lives.

The attitudes of others are contagious. A positive person can lift others up. The better you become, the more you attract incredible people. And the converse is also true. If you are negative, you will find a negative vortex around you. The power of people works both ways.

When it comes to knowing extraordinary people, I revel in my good fortune. My life has been shaped and guided by some incredible souls, both people brought into my life by pure fate—like my father—and those I have encountered while seeking to surround myself with only the most positive, talented, and inspiring people, like my business partners Mike and Blythe.

Do you actively seek to surround yourself with people who encourage your dreams and feed your positive mind-set? Who in your life makes you feel more certain about the future and yourself? Who inspires you to be a better version of yourself and helps you have a brighter vision of the world? Spend significantly more time with those people. The higher the quality of the people you surround yourself with, the better you become.

Involving others in your goals is a must. You grow from their expertise and resources; you escalate your own commitment; you keep yourself accountable—and you have a heck of a lot of fun together along the way.

the people who make us grow

Hands-down, my greatest influence is my father, Larry DiLullo, but you can call him The Great One. This is not a nickname I gave him; he actually requested that his kids call him this. We were also free to call him The Scientist! (said with flair). Despite his grandiose nicknames, my dad is one of the most humble and kind human beings you could ever meet, and he has always had a pretty great sense of humor.

Indulge me while I share a little background on The Great One—I promise, this detour has a point.

My father grew up in Connecticut with his mother and little brother. His father died when he was just three years old. During the summer between third and fourth grade, he convinced his mother that he could handle a paper route. He saw how hard she was working to get by, and he wanted to help out. After all, he was the man of the house. So my grandmother bought him a bicycle on installment payments, which he paid off with his profits. He delivered the paper to 130 customers after school and did such a good job on his first route that he won a day trip to Yankee Stadium. He kept the route until he was sixteen and could get a job bagging groceries twenty hours a week.

While he was always a hard worker, my dad was not always a good student. Knowing that he couldn't afford to go to college and that he was probably headed for a full-time job in a grocery store after he graduated, he had little motivation to study. In his senior year in high school, he earned a C-minus in trigonometry. Before the two-week holiday vacation, the teacher handed out the "Introduction to Calculus" textbooks and gave the class a little speech.

"If you thought trig was difficult, you don't know what difficult is. I'm not going to give you a passing grade in 'Introduction to Calculus' just because you're a graduating senior. If you flunk, you don't graduate."

Suddenly he was motivated. He couldn't imagine telling his mother he was not going to be the first in his family after all to graduate from high school. Over the holidays, he spent all day for two weeks going through every chapter, doing all the end-of-chapter problems until he nailed them.

Back in class after vacation, he went from "dunce" to "math genius." He scored 100 on all the tests and tells me now that he could have done a much better job teaching the course than the teacher did.

But his ambition did not stop there. That summer he went to the public library and borrowed two more books on differential calculus and continued to teach himself. Eventually, when he went to engineering school, he tested out and received credit for an advanced calculus course. All it took was a little motivation and lots of hours of concentration.

Later, when I was struggling in trig in high school and would ask my math genius father to help, he would just look at me and shake his head, throw his hands up in the air, and say, "Well, then, why don't you go out into the backyard and start practicing digging some ditches? What's the matter with you? You don't need my help. You need to crack a book!" (Drama is our strong suit in the DiLullo family.) Of course, I would be sitting there with an open book in front of me when he said this, but he knew I was not really applying myself. That was not his point. My dad taught me early on that it's all about effort. Don't ask someone else to be your crutch. Do the work. After all, why would you expect someone to show up and help you when you are not really showing up for yourself?

He lived this value every day. After high school, he worked at the grocery store full-time by day and went to a two-year state technical institute to get a degree in industrial engineering at night. His goal was always to get a better job so he could help his mother and little brother even more. He had a powerful *why* and was always willing to do the work to achieve it. And, even though he *had* to work to help not only himself but also his family at a very young age, he never looked at work as a chore.

My dad went on to get a full-time professional job as an industrial engineer, and on the side he became interested in home building. Once again he threw himself into his ambition. He signed up for a National Association of Home Builders seminar, subscribed to *American Builder* magazine, and read books on electrical wiring, plumbing, carpentry, and every other building trade. He learned how to do every trade himself and before long became so skilled that he and his cousin Joe built a home completely by themselves—and sold it—within a year. To do this he worked forty hours a week at nights and on weekends in addition to his full-time day job.

My dad married my mother, and then moved to Arizona and completed a master's degree in engineering while also working full-time. As soon as he was done with school he built two more houses on the side before he quit to do home building full-time. He was a very successful builder for seven years.

In the 1980s there was a great housing recession following the savings and loan debacle, and my dad was forced out of the construction business. The prime interest rate hit 20 percent, and many people could no longer afford home mortgages. As a comparison, as I write this, the prime rate is 3.25 percent. When the sales dried up, we went from living in a gorgeous home with a tennis court and swimming pool to living in a small apartment.

Yet my dad never seemed panicked or concerned; he never seemed to think this was a big deal at all. Having grown up with so much less, he knew just how well-off we still were. After all, we were healthy, and he was highly skilled and hardworking. His positivity rubbed off on his kids. When one of us would complain about something, he would reply, "So what? Tough luck!" All with a smile. On to the next thing.

Then, with his friend Barry, my dad started a small software company called Window on Wall Street, targeted at day traders. He coded, while his friend sold. How did he learn the latest programming languages? Well, he just picked up a few books and taught himself. There were always three or four technical manuals stacked up on every end table in our home.

Once the product was done, he sold out to his partner and moved us to California so he could set up a small computer development consulting company. He liked the freedom of working for himself with just a few other guys, as well as the variety of the work.

Though he routinely worked more than fifty hours a week, he always seemed to be around and willing to spend time with me at the drop of a hat. As much as he loved to work, he loved his kids infinitely more. I remember when my brother, sister, and I were little, on a scorching summer day in Arizona, we walked into his home office and said we wished we were at the beach. He said, "Okay. Get in the car." So we did. We drove six hours to California to go to the beach. He was a man who knew that being extraordinary wasn't just about succeeding professionally; showing up for family mattered even more.

My dad is also the kindest man I have ever met (tied with my husband). When my mother left, he never once said a bad word about her. If I groused about her, he would say something like, "That's your mother. Do you know your mother is excellent at sewing? She made you great Halloween costumes when you were little. You probably got your artistic skills from her." He *always* refocused on the positive and never joined in on harping on the negative.

He was not easily impressed, but always supportive. When I was competing in speech and debate competitions in places like Modesto, he would drive me the two hours each way to attend. When I was good at something, he was excessively proud. In fact, if you bump into him today, you might want to excuse yourself to use the bathroom before he regales you with stories of my triumphs of thirty years ago. He likes to act them out too—and in his performances my glory has only gotten greater as time has passed.

But when I was growing up, he never coddled me or gave big applause for what he viewed as minor accomplishments. When I graduated from high school, there was no party or presents. We walked to get frozen yogurt at Baskin-Robbins to celebrate. He said, "Oh, what's the big deal? Any kid that can fog a mirror can graduate high school."

He never worried about complimenting me to build my confidence, but instead encouraged me to cultivate that confidence within myself. I always felt his unconditional love, but he never told me I was good at something if I was not, and he never did anything for me that I was capable of doing for myself. Had he, do you think I would be as resilient as I am today? I don't think so.

Today, he comes to every sales conference we have, simply to, as he puts it, watch me in action. He also makes other relatives come. People who sit near him always report back to me that my dad was talking the whole time. And since he is hard of hearing, he has a tendency to shout. "Isn't she great!? Just look at her!"

My role model for a parent was not someone who hovered over me, watching my every move or worrying about my perfectly balanced nutrition. My dad was too busy seeing the bigger picture.

My dad—who he is, where he came from, how he built his life—was the absolutely perfect role model for me. It's essentially because of him that I came to understand just what the entrepreneurial spirit is all about. From him I learned about the value of hard work to take you anywhere you want to go. I learned the power of a positive mind-set and the need for resilience. I also learned how risk and failure are just part of success.

All I've got to say is this: when choosing the people to support you on your journey to extraordinary, you should strive to surround yourself with people like Larry. I have always considered my dad the world's greatest parent. All three of his children love him beyond measure and will say that, without a doubt, he actually deserves to be called The Great One.

lessons from the great one

- FAMILY FIRST. YOU ALWAYS TAKE CARE OF YOUR FAMILY. My dad is a veritable tyrant in this regard.
- YES, YOU CAN AFFORD TO LEARN AND GROW. Get a second job if you need to and cut everything else. Don't ever skimp on your own education. Nor should you ever have to. My dad would say the public library has books and the Internet, and it's all free.
- WANT TO LEARN SOMETHING? CRACK A BOOK. Larry never thought that not knowing how to do something was a deterrent to getting started, nor did he need someone else's

stamp of approval to certify him as ready or complete. He was always curious, and even today, at seventy-eight, he's always learning something new.

- WORK HARD AND TAKE PRIDE IN YOUR WORK. My dad took pride in everything he did, whether it was bagging groceries, developing computer software, or parenting.
- IF YOU DON'T LIKE WHAT YOU'RE DOING, JUST FIX IT. WHAT'S THE BIG DEAL? GO DO SOMETHING YOU LIKE. My dad would never linger doing something he didn't love. He reinvented his career several times.
- BE GENEROUS AND KIND. TO EVERYBODY.

dominoes and linchpins

Stella & Dot may have started in my living room, but that is not how it was created. After all, an idea is pretty worthless without other people to help you make it real. Some of the people who have come along have played temporary or small parts in the story, but they were critical dominoes. Who knows which domino changed the trajectory of the company? Every single member of our home office team and our sales field, and every single customer, played a part in our success.

In the very beginning, when I was still living in Texas but planning to move out to California to really start the company, I reached out with a cold call to Janice Parsons, the owner of a popular bead shop in Palo Alto. Janice provided services and space for us in the basement of her office off Emerson Street in Palo Alto. She was an essential domino.

Around that same time, a friend of a friend called me to ask me for advice on his start-up and to see whether I would be interested in coming to work there. I offered advice, but said no-thank-you on the job. I told him what I was working on. He kindly introduced me to his friend Maya Brenner, a celebrity jewelry designer. Maya played a big role in taking the jewelry I had been making, all beaded stones, and making it *a lot* cooler. Her Charmed Life Necklace became our best-seller and was seen on tons of celebrities, providing some critical exposure that helped us take the business to a new level.

When I was ready to really grow Luxe Jewels, I reached out to Doug Mackenzie at Radar Partners, the same investor who had been on my board at WeddingChannel.com. Even more than I needed the seed capital, I needed his bright mind and his supportive voice, always challenging me to do better and think bigger. Doug has an uncanny knack for asking the right questions.

Doug and his partners didn't know anything about the industry, but he believed in me from our time working together at WeddingChannel.com, three years earlier. Not too many investor pitches start out saying, "Look, I have a baby now, and I will likely have another soon, so I am going to pace this around my young family. Oh, and I don't want to take the company public. I want to keep control of the company so I can keep the focus on the mission. Our priority will not be hyper-growth and profit by the quarter. Our metrics of success are going to be our impact. I can't tell you exactly how fast we'll get there, but I do know there is something big here. What do you think?"

Like I said, it was not a typical investor pitch. At least, not a typical successful one. But Doug is far from a typical investor. He invests in people. He simply said, "If you're in, I'm in."

Eighteen months later, after I'd had my second daughter and was ready to pick up the pace, I put a notice on a business school alumni message board asking if anyone had a connection to someone who had worked in direct sales. Someone who worked at WeddingChannel.com recognized my name and connected me to Mike Lohner, another alum, who had most recently been the CEO of a billion-dollar direct sales company.

After an hour of conversation on the phone, I told Mike I was getting on a plane to see him the next day. When we met, I explained that my baby, Tatum, was only six months old, so my priority was running this business around my family, and that I needed help. While I couldn't yet pay him, I asked him to invest, telling him that together we would not do small and we would not do good—we would do big and we would do great! I would work my hardest to make it the best business decision he ever made. Thankfully, he said yes.

Mike became an investor and my partner in March 2007. He is a very active chairman who has been full-time and part-time over the years but has always put Stella & Dot first. He taught me almost everything I know about direct selling. Most important, he's an inspiration for how to be an amazing human.

Good people attract good people. When Mike Lohner joined Luxe Jewels, it got the attention of the top Canadian leader in his previous company, Danielle Redner—yes, the dairy farmer's wife turned trainer extraordinaire you read about earlier. She told Mike that she wanted to do what he was doing. He introduced us, and she then tracked me down and asked if we were expanding to Canada. We were barely in the United States! It made no strategic sense for us to expand that quickly. And yet, after a one-hour phone call with her, I knew this woman was amazing. Mike and I both believed that it was worth opening up a country just to get a chance to work with her. So we did. Best decision we ever made—Danielle is *that* extraordinary.

With Mike and Danielle on board, our team was coming

together, but a key linchpin was still missing. Our charm necklace was by far our best-seller, and at our jewelry-making parties people often picked the artisan-made option. But painstakingly handmade jewelry is hard to scale, and the DIY experience is not for everyone. The business was growing, but it was going to grow much faster if we focused on offering only very stylish and affordable ready-made jewelry. Next, I needed a full-time partner in mid-market accessory design.

At a football tailgater at his ten-year college reunion, Chad reconnected with a former classmate, Blythe Henwood Harris. What had she been up to? She was most recently developing Banana Republic's jewelry business. What a coincidence! He suggested she meet with his wife.

Blythe kindly took the meeting, even though she suspected it was another jewelry designer trying to pitch designs to be sold at Banana Republic. We first met in the GAP cafeteria for lunch. Blythe had a tremendously impressive background. I knew she could really help take the company to a completely different level.

Given that Blythe was about to get married and was in a "dream job," it took a year of courtship for Blythe to join forces with us (a true lesson in the power of persistence).

Blythe is an extreme outlier in her creative talents and accomplishments, but that was not the sole reason I was certain she was the right partner. Blythe is one of the greatest people you could ever meet. She's funny, sweet, brilliant, and passionate. It was her belief in our company's mission of helping other women that ultimately won her over.

As an entrepreneur, Blythe was passionate about using her talents to reinvent retail as she knew it. She knew firsthand about the opportunities in the mid-market jewelry space and about the limitations of having pieces locked up in a glass case in a retail store.

Blythe not only joined our company as the chief creative officer, but invested in the business and became a partner. Together we renamed the company Stella & Dot after our beloved grandmothers.

We are true partners in the sense that we are just better together. We work closely together to conceive each of our brands, pouring our passion into every element of those businesses from all we've learned and dreamed about over the last eight years of our partnership.

There is no doubt that Stella & Dot would not be what it is today without all of the dominoes and all of the linchpins. The point is that any success I have created has always been the sum of my own efforts plus the efforts of all those I've been surrounded by— people far more talented than I at what they do—and the great love, trust, and respect we've developed for one another.

My first business partner, Jenny, once joked with me about a documentary on Siegfried & Roy in which they discussed their partnership, both in life and in the ring. Who is the magician and who is the magic, they asked? Jenny and I couldn't figure out the answer to this question either, but in our best German accents we still liked to tell each other, "No, *you* are the magic!" To this day I think *all* the people I have had the privilege to work alongside are the magic.

How do you feel about the people you surround yourself with and share goals with? Don't just partner with those you bump into. Pursue the best. Actively seek those you think are magic.

don't let the naysayers sit in your front row

Oscar Wilde once said, "Never love anyone who treats you like you're ordinary." So true. To see how extraordinary you are you

Don't let
naysayers
sit in your
front row.

need to be around the people who already see extraordinary in you. We've all been around naysayers and negative people. They may not be bad people, but for the time and place you are in you find that they drag you down instead of lift you up. When you choose who gets to be in your life, choose wisely.

Naysayers will always exist, but you don't have to let them sit in your front row. At times I've had naysayers around, and it brought down both of us, as well as the other people around us. Moving on from those situations is often difficult, but always better for everybody. I've had to learn the hard way how negative it can be to allow negative people to stick around.

Sometimes it's crystal clear when you have a toxic person situation going on. I've had my fair share of these, like the drunken accountant, the dishonest HR team member, the employee who committed theft, you name it. People, even good people, can behave badly. And at times our culture and our work environments are not the best and probably play a role in driving them to behave badly. There are always two sides to the story. Regardless, when someone steals from you, or is dishonest, or does something to threaten the success of your business, deciding whether or not to keep them around tends to be a very cut-and-dry choice.

What you need to be careful of, though, are those people who have lots to love about them but are nevertheless dragging you and the people around you down. How do you spot such a person? After you spend time with this kind of naysayer, you generally feel less inspired, less energetic, less positive. You focus on problems, not solutions. This person has a negative mind-set that lures your brain right into its vortex. Misery loves company.

You don't need to assign blame; there's no need to label this person a bad person. He or she is probably a great person in a bad place. However, that doesn't mean this person gets to keep sitting in your front row. You have to distance yourself from those who hold you back.

This is not about abandoning a friend or family member in need. This is not about labeling a person who is having a bad day as a negative person. I'm talking about not discussing your new venture with the person who seems to find fault in much of what you do. I'm talking about going out to lunch less often with the coworker who is *always* complaining about his boss instead of passionately talking about what he is working on. I'm talking about spending less time with the friend who *always* seems to be criticizing others or having yet another conflict with someone. And certainly, if you are in a relationship with someone who *often* cuts *you* down, you need to fix that. Immediately.

find the good in others

No one is perfect, and people are not always 100 percent lovable. Even in the best of times, our friends, family, partners, and coworkers can rub us the wrong way or do the wrong things. This is not the type of person you distance yourself from, rather you diminish your own negative reaction to them in these moments. To avoid being negative about people, which gets you nowhere, try picturing that person as a child. I'm not kidding. For an instant, imagine him or her at their most vulnerable. I choose to believe that most people are filled with tremendous good. If they are expressing negative traits, their attitude or behaviors are most likely coming from insecurity or a need for recognition, love, or fulfillment. So you have a choice: You can shine a light on their negative traits, no doubt helping the negativity grow. Or you can seek out their positive traits, which probably aren't hard to find if you take the time to look.

become the leader you want to follow

Whether you run a company or a household, even if you have no official leadership position at all, you *are* a leader and the world is awaiting your instructions. You don't need to be in a top box on an organizational chart or president of the PTA or your sorority to be a leader. Regardless of your current role or position, you are always leading the people around you. You lead long before you have a title that spells it out. So today recognize and take responsibility for the influence you have on others and focus on lifting up the people around you.

I know that I am my greatest source of strength, but I also know that I shine brighter when I turn the light on others. Entrepreneurs have *giant* hero complexes, but let's not blame ourselves too harshly. Starting out, there used to be no one else who could possibly do that task better than us—because in fact there was no one else! But then, if we did our jobs well, we grew and we hired others, and then we had to evolve our definition of success. It was now no longer about doing everything but about developing and delegating to others so that we could continue to move our venture forward.

At WeddingChannel.com, I struggled with this. We raised more than $40 million in venture capital and we went from two employees to over 140 in a year, and I suddenly found myself in a position of leadership for which I was ill prepared.

My priority was to deliver things and meet customer and investor expectations; otherwise, we would go out of business and all the employees would lose their jobs. The metrics of success were all about eyeballs, not profitability. It felt like a mad race down the rabbit hole—and it was. It was an intense time in the market, and

You are a leader
and the world is
awaiting your
instructions.

finally there was a reckoning for the irrational exuberance that took over Silicon Valley and overfunded every bad-idea.com with a ridiculous valuation. Massive layoffs started happening all around us. On the one hand, it was a great time to buy Aeron chairs and Ping-Pong tables on eBay. On the other, it was a challenging time to be a leader.

At twenty-four years old, I didn't yet have the emotional intelligence that comes with life experience. Instead of encouraging and inspiring the people around me, I just drove us harder and raised the bar higher. I often micromanaged every detail and thought that most things were not good enough. I worked all the time, and I didn't understand why all of my colleagues did not show the same kind of overzealous work ethic.

I can proudly say that our business did survive, and it *did* work, but I am not proud of my leadership through it all. Times of pressure are the times when a leader needs to be at her best, not her worse. The leader has the greatest impact on everyone else in the group, and people need to be lifted up, not torn down.

If you find yourself in a difficult situation, my advice is to consider who needs your leadership. Your family, your team, your community? Think about what the view looks like from where others are standing. Think about what they need in order to get to a better place. Be the leader you want to follow.

be you

When we first started thinking about global expansion for Stella & Dot, I wanted to be sure that our products and sales methods would work as well for the European woman as they did in North America. So I went back to the beginning and started reaching out to anyone who knew anyone in London and tried to book some test trunk shows so I could experience firsthand what this expansion would take to succeed.

When I landed, I met with our barrister (European for lawyer) to talk about some of the legal elements of our expansion. I explained to her that we were in the service business, not just in sales. Our Stylists focus on offering every guest personal suggestions. As we parted ways, and right before I was hopping into a taxi to go to my first show, she gave me some advice. "British women are far more reserved. You wouldn't want to be too suggestive here. She won't like that. That's very American. Just let her be."

Uh-oh. Was I about to be the stereotypical obnoxious American? I never pressure a guest to shop, but I also want to make sure she leaves with ideas on which accessories work best with her personal style, coloring, and body type. In my experience, women love that!

When I arrived at my first British trunk show, I heeded the barrister's advice. I barely gave an introduction and just let the women browse. Then I saw a woman, with dazzling blue eyes, looking a bit bewildered by all the options. So I said to the crowd, somewhat sheepishly, "Now, anyone with blue eyes might really look good in this necklace because it would make those eyes just pop!" Then I just started laughing at how absurd I sounded. Screw it. I was just going to be myself and do what I do.

To explain my sudden burst of laughter, I said, "Ladies, I have to confess! I was told by my barrister not to style you. But I can't help it. I'm staring at Melissa, who I just met, with the gorgeous blue eyes, and I'm dying to see her in this turquoise necklace! You can tell me if being this direct is no good for you, but I want to give you what I think is the best Stella & Dot experience, and that involves telling you exactly which pieces you need to look cuter. Then will you please help me by giving me your honest feedback? I really need your help to figure out this coming from America thing!"

As soon as I became myself I began to have fun. As I began to have fun everyone else did too. And guess what? I sold over $17,000 in accessories in three days at five trunk shows. How do you think that would have gone if I had tried to be someone else?

What I have found is that as much as there may be cultural differences across borders, what women have in common is greater than what sets them apart. They love to hang out with other women, and they get joy from feeling confident when they love the way they look. And most of all, they connect with each other best when they are simply being authentic.

I've now done trunk shows and trainings in Germany, France, Ireland, Canada, and the United Kingdom. Our products change slightly by country, but *I* don't change.

I have learned that whenever I feel uncomfortable or awkward, I just admit it and try to diffuse the situation with honesty, humor, and a little vulnerability. Why sit there and struggle alone? Others appreciate your honesty and want to help you when you ask for it. You can't try to mimic someone else. Inauthentic is unappealing and terribly ordinary. You'll never be extraordinary unless you are comfortable with and proud of who you are.

five traits of an extraordinary leader

1. BE BENEVOLENT: Have an authentic interest in helping people be their best.
2. HAVE MORE THAN A WORK ETHIC—SHOW A TRUE LOVE FOR YOUR WORK: If you're the leader, you're the pacesetter in the race. And remember, winning a race means

running hard and often requires a sprint to the finish. Don't expect others to do or care more than you do. Show up. Show up. Show up.

3. BE AUDACIOUSLY GOAL-ORIENTED: You only get what you go after, so be bold, be specific, and share your goals with others. Paint a bull's-eye for yourself and your team.

4. BE POSITIVE, BE CONFIDENT, AND DIMINISH DRAMA: Set the right tone. When you are both positive and confident, others will pick up your vibe and be willing to follow. Shine the light on what you want to grow, which is progress and passion, not drama. Never talk *about* people, talk *to* people. Ensure that others do the same.

5. BE AUTHENTIC AND SELF-AWARE: You need to be you. But you also need to respect other people's individual beliefs and be aware of how they are experiencing you. You can be your authentic self while still being respectful of others. Don't try to use "authenticity" as an excuse for being a jerk.

6. CARE MORE ABOUT MAKING IT RIGHT: When it comes to people, it's not about being right, it's about making it right. I am not talking about the difference between true right and wrong. Clearly, it's important to be in the right, ethically speaking. I am talking about letting go of the useless "I told you so" or "I just want to prove how smart I am" type of being right.

lift people up

If you want to go fast, go alone.
If you want to go far, go together.
—AFRICAN PROVERB

Making a conscious choice to lift others up is an essential part of being a great leader. And while that sounds good, and rather obvious, leadership ain't easy. That's for sure. You lead the people around you every day, whether you know it or not, whether you like it or not. This responsibility might feel like a burden at times— that is, until you get over yourself and realize what a privilege it is to influence others. Isn't that what it's all about? To feel that in this life you don't just pass by people, but that you shape their lives and they shape yours?

I don't get it all right, all the time, not by a mile. But I try. After I had my babies to get home to, I was always focused on being uber-efficient in my workday. Part of what made me good at what I did was my ability to get a wide variety of things done quickly. But I was never going to be extraordinary that way. I was too focused on getting it done, and not focused enough on being the kind of leader others wanted to follow. For example, if someone wasn't getting to what I thought was the right answer fast enough, I'd give it to him or her and move on. This also created the problem of others going directly to me to get something done, versus going to others who were quite capable to resolve a situation. I spent too much time doing and too little time building our company through building people.

It took years, but ultimately I shifted my focus away from "what did I get done in that sixty-minute meeting?" to "did I develop others and how did people on my team feel when I left the room?"

I never lowered the bar for excellence, nor did I ask less of my team and myself. We still play to win at Stella & Dot. I just became a heck of a lot more effective at how I pass the ball.

There are still times when my communication style is lacking—usually when I've been traveling too much and sleeping too little. When I'm in one time zone answering questions from people in another, I'm tired and my answers can get curt. I've learned to really check my reactions and responses when I am in that situation. I have now learned to not go into the office immediately after I've gotten straight off a flight and have been in three cities in three days. I have also learned to eliminate late-night email. When you are face-to-face, calmly offering direct feedback, you can inspire someone to be and do much better.

Now, I still don't get that right every day, but I do a lot more often than I used to. We are *all* works in progress. As Coco Chanel so astutely said, "I am nothing but flaws stitched together with good intention."

Lifting people up makes the world a better place. Sure, you'd feel better about the "make the world a better place" claim if you were going to cure cancer or fix global warming, but in case that is not on your short-term to-do list, why not take small steps and focus on making a tiny impact on just the people you come into contact with in your daily life? It takes you zero extra time and probably saves you time because you have to deal with less drama. Making a few people just a tiny bit happier each day—that is a better world.

Start by Regularly Asking Yourself, "How Did I Make People Feel Today?"
- Generally, when you leave a room, how do people feel? Energized and excited? Focused and clear? Or criticized

We are all
works in progress.

and corrected? Dazed and confused? Bored? Negative? Or do they even remember you were in it?

- When a coworker asked you a question, were you really listening, or were you checking email on your phone?

- When you were chatting with someone at a party, did you ask her a question about herself with genuine interest, or were you looking around in case someone more interesting came in? Or were you not really listening, waiting to talk about yourself?

- When your spouse got home from work, did you stop what you were doing and look him or her in the eye while you connected about the day?

- Did you create a memory with your child, even if it was a tiny moment?

When you are not thrilled with the answers to these questions, don't get frustrated—get curious. You are human and no matter how awesome you are, you will not always be your best. When you stay in a positive mind and get curious about what caused you to not be your best, you can turn it around more quickly. Was it an impulsive action aided by alcohol? Were you tired from a lack of sleep? Or stressed from a lack of exercise? Change and control those circumstances and show up better next time.

commiseration is for the ordinary

Today, everyone is in the broadcast business. People post on social media, employees "reply all," friends "like" and "share" in Facebook groups, and middle schoolers participate in big group texts that create a near constant buzz on their phones every night. All of these exchanges are forms of social broadcasts. In fact in today's social-media-driven culture, it's tempting to communicate with a large group of people, in an instant, instead of having a direct conversation with just one person. And all without really thinking about the messages we are sending.

When you broadcast, consider the audience. It's easy to forget that when you post on social media or broadcast a message to all, you're essentially grabbing a mic and taking the stage.

Think, for a moment, about the type of broadcast you are creating. It's natural to share our daily experiences, both positive and negative. When you have a problem or something negative to share, consider if it really needs to be said at all. If it does, share it privately, with the fewest number of people who can help you solve it. If you are ever sharing a problem, be sure you are seeking a solution, not just commiseration. After all, commiseration requires that someone else be miserable too. Is that what you want to be known for?

learning how to listen

Both my mind and my mouth can start moving at 100 miles per hour. At my worst, this passion and expressiveness can drown out other voices, and I end up taking up more than my fair share of space in the conversation. In these moments, I lose the value of learning. We all have two ears and one mouth and should use them in that order.

Go through your day and see how often you *really* listened to someone. Were you truly focused on what they were saying, or were you too busy thinking about how you were going to respond? I learned the value of really listening in an exercise with a group of executives at a retreat. We formed pairs, and the objective was to simply let your partner talk for three uninterrupted minutes about what "was important to you and on your mind right now." I paired up with my friend Dave Goldberg, a serial entrepreneur and the CEO of SurveyMonkey. One of Dave's superpowers was his innate people skills, and he had given me many great leadership insights over the years.

While we listened, we were to not respond and to try not to be thinking about a response—the whole idea was to say *nothing* next. So I just looked my friend in the eyes and listened as he talked. How much nicer it was, I discovered, to give that person the gift of my focus and energy instead of my comments. And without distraction, it was much easier for me to truly hear what he was saying.

When someone starts sharing, it's natural to want to jump in and ask clarifying questions. It's not interrupting, it's curiosity, right? Well, no, it's still interrupting. But it's offering empathy, which is kind, right? Well, no, switching to a story about how you too felt that way once is also still interrupting. When you force yourself to say nothing and just let another person keep going, it allows that person to go to a much deeper place and be more authentic.

At the end of the three-minute exercise, I knew something real about my partner that six months of cocktail parties and superficial conversation would have never unearthed. In 180 seconds, what started out as my friend's story about the logistics of arranging for a parent to come visit turned into sharing his feelings around the loss of his other parent, expressing his concerns about living far away from his mother, and recognizing his desire for them to live closer to each other.

I realized that if we had not been doing this exercise, early in the conversation when he mentioned his mother, I probably would have asked, "Oh, really? Where does she live? How often do you go visit?" It might have turned into a conversation about trivialities instead of feelings. Had I done any of that, I would have never heard the depth of his emotion and thoughts. I would have inadvertently taken over the direction of what had the potential to be an extraordinary interaction and driven it to a very ordinary place.

When it was my turn to talk, I felt relaxed and connected. I was blown away by the quality of exchange you can have in only six minutes. If pictures are worth a thousand words, truly listening to someone is worth one million of your own words.

I am not suggesting that you act like a strange psychoanalyst and change all of your conversational contributions to "Mmm-hmmm, tell me more about that." Just sharpen your awareness of how much space you take up in conversations.

Shortly after that three-minute conversation, that friend passed away. I wish I could get another three minutes. He was the kind of guy who knew how to really listen to people long before that exercise. But I will make sure that, in his honor, I never forget the power of listening more than talking and of striving to make sure everyone I talk to feels truly heard.

haters gonna hate, but makers gonna make

In the early days of Stella & Dot, I had a baby and a toddler. When people asked what my hobbies were, I would laugh. Coloring, Dora the Explorer, Polly Pocket dolls, and watching every animated film fifty times. So it will come as no surprise that one of my favorite quotes about leadership comes from the movie *A Bug's Life*. Hopper, the attacking grasshopper, says to the Princess Ant, "The first rule of leadership, Princess: it's *always* your fault."

That kind of pressure can make leadership seem *very* unappealing, right? As long as you learn not to feel so much pressure that you scurry around like an ant under the shadow of a shoe, leadership can be great.

As a leader, if you are overly defensive or sensitive and don't like getting feedback, you are going to limit your growth. If you want to be extraordinary, you need to get on board with toughening up.

Take the pressure off. Remember, we are all works in progress, and you are never going to get it all right, all the time, with all the people. You have to try to be better, but you also have to be willing to own up to screwing up when that happens, and accepting it's not the end of the world.

I tend to welcome the blame for a situation or relationship gone wrong because it's part of my personality type—I want to think I can be in control of my life. I like to think I caused the bad things because, that way, I can change them rather than being at the mercy of others. So I generally take 110 percent responsibility for anything that goes wrong.

Constructive criticism is never fun to hear, but if you accept it with an open mind, it goes a long way toward making you a better leader. I have looked for the kernels of truth in the critical feedback I've gotten and have found *plenty* of valid points I can work with. A good clue is when you see a theme emerging from many people, versus one-off complaints from people who generally complain a lot.

Some feedback is valid, and some may not be. My extreme aversion to having a victim's mentality had me in denial over the fact that people tend to criticize female leaders more than they criticize male leaders. Yet, in some moments, I do wonder: if I were a man, would I be called "strong" and "decisive" instead of "demanding" and "aggressive"?

There is no doubt that when you're a leader in a dress, people seem more taken aback by a strong personality type. I try to say what I mean without being mean, but I get to the point and I do speak my mind.

I have also accepted that if you are going to step out front, you may take a few bullets. But it's up to you to decide how real those bullets are and how much they hurt you. In other words, haters gonna hate, but makers gonna make.

extraordinary ways to communicate with people

- BE PRESENT IN THE MOMENT YOU ARE IN: Listen. More than you talk.
- CLEAR THE AIR: If you're uncomfortable in a situation, candidly and kindly voice your thoughts. Something like "You know, I feel funny even saying this, but I left that conversa-

tion with a strange feeling. The story I am telling myself is
_____, but what are your thoughts?"

- DON'T GOSSIP: Talk to people, not about people. But be sure you say what you mean without *being* mean.

- PAUSE AND LISTEN: When you make your point, pause and wait. Too often people keep going, nervously chattering away. Get comfortable with a little silence. Often, if you pause and listen, someone will ask you a question or reveal an insight that takes the conversation in a more useful and interesting direction.

- JUDGE PEOPLE ON THEIR INTENTIONS, NOT ONLY ON THEIR ACTIONS: If you do this, you'll be more kind and forgiving. And the more you are forgiving and understanding, the more people will return the favor when you need it.

- RECOGNIZE THE WORK OF OTHERS: Recognition is the most powerful currency you have, and it costs you nothing. Catch someone doing something good and acknowledge it out loud and, better yet, in front of others. Conversely, if you catch someone doing something bad, do not call it out in front of others. Doing that may be quicker and more efficient, but it is not harmless.

- BE YOU: If you speak your mind, not everyone will love you—and that is okay. If you are aiming for universal affection, you'll be plain vanilla, not the real you. The real you is *loved* by 80 percent of the people around you and is much better than the watered-down you—the one 100 percent of the people around you describe as *all right*.

CHAPTER 7

perseverance

I'ma rip this shit till my bones collapse.
—EMINEM

EARLY IN MY CAREER AS AN ENTREPRENEUR, I thought that if I ever wrote a book, it would be in the voice of Dr. Seuss: "Problems here, problems there, problems everywhere!" It's true: my road to success has been paved with failures, setbacks, and every flavor of problem under the sun.

If you've committed to following your authentic passions down a path to create something truly meaningful, with a positive mindset and the support of people who will help you make it happen, congratulations. You're well on your way to creating an extraordinary life. But there's more. Without stamina, you'll tucker out before you arrive. That's why you need extraordinary perseverance to fuel you on your journey.

Dreaming big is great. But you still need a work ethic and a will that is at least as big as your dreams. Never assume that success is set aside for the predetermined few who always have the wind at their back. Nor is success only for those who never fall down. Success is simply for those who persevere—those who get back up, dust themselves off, and try all over again.

Does that mean that if you want to succeed, you can't ever quit anything? Not exactly. When my daughter Tatum wanted to stop taking piano lessons, she came to me and said, "Mom, I don't want to be a quitter, but I really want to quit." I knew how she felt. We all want to quit lots of things, all the time. And some things you *should* quit. If there's something you don't really care about, something that you are not willing to make trade-offs for, then go ahead, quit that thing. In fact, focusing on something extraordinary requires eliminating the not-so-important things from your life. You have to live your life in accordance with your values and your goals. It's totally okay to quit the rest.

But first you have to decide what is on your "do not quit" list. For me, quality time with my family and the success of my business are at the top of my "do not quit" list. Even in the early days of Luxe Jewels, when success looked dubious to others, I knew it was a certainty. Why? I had eliminated giving up as an option. To make that happen, though, I had to quit lots of other, less important things.

Here's one example. My husband and I have always wished we were more musical. So, for Chad's birthday one year, I bought us guitars and hired a rocker by the name of Groovy Judy (seriously, that was her name!) to give us weekly lessons. Every Wednesday at 9:00 PM, after we put our kids to bed, we had rehearsal time for our rock band, Chassica. (Clever, right?) Turned out, Chad was actually pretty good. I, on the other hand, was terrible.

After a few months, I had learned how to play exactly half of one Green Day song—"Boulevard of Broken Dreams." How appropriate. Then Groovy Judy fired me because it was evident I practiced zero times in between my lessons. In truth, it was a relief. Did I think guitar playing was cool? Yes. Was Groovy Judy truly groovy? Yes. Did learning to play the guitar really matter to me? No.

What went wrong? I wasn't willing to persevere at learning how to play guitar, so I became a quitter. This was a wise move for me because I needed to quit guitar in order to succeed at what mattered much more to me—my start-up business. Whatever spare time I had after taking care of my family, I wanted to spend getting a bit more work done, not practicing guitar.

Pick what matters to you, and then be happy with that choice. Don't let feeling bad about what you did not choose stand in the way of getting joy from focusing on what you want most. Life goals shouldn't feel like a shopping list where you just roll down an aisle and toss things in the cart. To be extraordinary, you'll have to accept trade-offs. I, for one, am comfortable with the idea that I could go to my grave without ever playing the second half of that song.

Just be careful you don't tell yourself it's okay to quit something you truly want to accomplish, though I get why you'd be tempted to do this. You are scared you won't be able to make it happen, so you don't set big goals. You hesitate. You talk in caveats. You set the bar low, and guess what happens? You hit it. But wouldn't you rather give yourself the chance to be awesome by persevering long enough to hit a high bar?

Your goals *should* feel uncomfortable. They *should* be things you have to persevere at. They should feel like, "Wow, I don't know exactly how I am going to make this happen, but how extraordinary it would be if I did!" Then you get to work figuring out how.

Recently, a young friend of mine was disappointed that she didn't land a spot on a competitive dance team. Taking this as a sign that she was never going to be good enough, she was tempted to quit. I told her she was simply experiencing the key ingredient she needed to be a winner: the willingness to lose. I know I am a winner only because I have lost more than most. Being an occasional loser at something is actually a good thing! When you are at risk of losing, you know you are competing at the right level, a level of true challenge.

I think our society in general is much too obsessed with the notion of everyone is a winner. In particular, I believe we've gone overboard on ensuring that no kids are ever losers. We are overly concerned that losing a soccer game or a mock trial debate will be an irreparable hit to kids' self-esteem. This is nuts. I think the far greater concern should be the outcome of coddling children: taking away their ability to persevere. I assume that my children are strong enough to deal with defeat, and that's the way it should be. Losing is an essential life skill. Kids need to learn to deal with the fact that everyone does not get a ribbon all the time. Yes, losing sucks. You don't like the way it feels? Try harder. Do better next time. That's how you become extraordinary. When did the definition of good parenting overcorrect to doing everything for and giving everything to our children? Even though I make my children do for themselves, I still wonder if their greatest disadvantage will be all their advantages. I do not want my doting to rob them of their own capabilities. Most of the time, I tell them: if you want something, go get it; it will not come to you. And I do not want my accomplishments to rob them of their own hunger. I know my children will need to struggle on their own to get stronger.

At the summer camp I am no longer sending my kids to, everyone is a winner. Everyone gets a ribbon. When my friend Jenny, who is also very pro-losing, called around to find some great summer camps for her kids, her first question actually was: "Does your camp have any losers? Yes? Great, please tell me more."

Ask yourself this. When you are making your way along your path, you experience a setback, and you feel like quitting, is it because the goal doesn't really matter to you, or are you just being way too fragile? Don't just assume that switching to a new path will suddenly make things easier or you may find that you are in the business of switching rather than succeeding. Summon up that entrepreneurial spirit so that you can be curious and committed instead of frustrated. Most of the time you simply need to persevere.

you are stronger than you know

I have been privileged to witness ordinary people creating extraordinary lives, despite challenging circumstances. Their successes came down to their ability to tap into their personal strength and persevere.

Take Cindy, for example. Cindy was exactly who you think of when you picture a forty-something stay-at-home mom living in Ohio. She was married with three daughters, ages nine, eleven, and fourteen, when she became a Stella & Dot Stylist. She had previously spent her days running her household, carpooling her girls to their sports, and being involved in their schools. "We were a typical All-American family from the Midwest," she said, "with my husband being the breadwinner and me a very active, content, stay-at-home mom." Then one day two years into her career, her husband, who worked in commercial real estate, came home and told her that his company was involved in a civil lawsuit. Cindy thought to herself, *We can deal with him getting another job. He's so good at what he does.*

But then things took an ugly turn. The civil lawsuit turned into a criminal trial. The day of the sentencing the police took her husband into custody and sent him to prison for eight years. Overnight her ideal family life turned into a version of hell that Cindy couldn't even recognize.

Some weak choices on Cindy's part would have been understandable, given the drastic change in her circumstances. She could have become angry, bitter, and resentful. She could have wallowed in the grave injustice done to her and her daughters. She could have run away from that town and that community. But she did none of those things. Instead, she focused on how she could make the best possible life for her daughters and herself while her husband (yes, she stayed committed to her marriage) was in prison.

In five years, Cindy earned over $1 million from launching and growing her own business with Stella & Dot. Not only did she become the sole provider, but she paid their mortgage, all their bills, and began paying for her two daughters' college tuitions. After those five years, Cindy's husband became eligible for judicial release. When he got out, he found a very different—and more extraordinary—wife greeting him at the prison gates. "It hasn't been an easy road, and we are certainly no longer a traditional family," she said, "but I would have never realized how to believe in myself and my own strength if my life hadn't changed so radically overnight."

Amazingly, over this same time period, Cindy also went through a personal transformation, losing twenty-five pounds. She realized along the way that she needed to care not only for her girls but also for herself. She transformed her diet, switching to clean eating, and found she had more energy than ever before.

I often find that people who accomplish something they would not have imagined for themselves in one area of their lives start to see that success overflow into other areas. Cindy tapped into a well of strength that she'd always had, and the water, as it turned out, ran deep.

You also have a well of strength. And you don't have to wait for a crisis to use it. You don't have to save it up. In fact, the more you tap into your well of strength, the deeper it gets. Why not tap into that well now? As you go about your daily life, do you bring your full strength to bear? If not, what are you waiting for?

The more
you tap into
your well
of strength,
the deeper
it gets.

When you are successful and you have accomplished things that seem extraordinary, people tend to assume that all of your stars were always aligned and that your road to success was smooth and easy. This couldn't be further from the truth. When I have had the privilege of meeting highly successful people and learning about their lives, I can't help but note just how many have had to overcome personal hardships that required them to be resilient. They are successful not because they never faced adversity, but because in that moment of hardship they dove into the well of their own strength. Who knows what critical lesson you will take from adversity that will strengthen you into who you are about to become?

I can look back at the adversity I have faced and see the strength that has come from it. That's a choice you have with every challenge. My mother had her own struggles, and that created a less than ideal upbringing for her three kids. Yet I see that as one of the key factors that instilled resilience in me. Once you realize you can survive a very difficult circumstance, you realize how powerful you truly are.

to persevere, you need perspective

Whenever I am feeling a bit sorry for myself, I try to get perspective so I can remind myself that actually my life is not that hard. Others have persevered under far more dire conditions. Looking back into my own family has the double benefit of reminding me not only of what others have endured but of what my gene pool has endured to get here. Surely I have inherited some of that resilience. Stella, my maternal grandmother, was a fantastic fireball of a woman. She raised five kids and was very loving and strong. Truth be told, I was lucky on both sides of the family. I have always been inspired by the life and strength of my paternal grandmother, Angelina Rosa Sica DiLullo.

Can you tell that my grandma Angie was Italian? She could have come right out of central casting for a Nona. She stood about five feet tall and wore a dress, suntan-colored pantyhose, and lipstick every day into her nineties. And she had lots of plastic figurines of the Virgin Mary. When she was older and lived with my dad, we'd give her flowers for Mother's Day, and the kind she liked always came with a little plastic Jesus or Mary. She'd collect them and put them on doilies on her dresser, like any good Italian grandmother would do. Occasionally, my dad would try to declutter and toss them, and she would yell, "Larry! What's the matter with you? You don't throw away God!" She was a great woman. Strong in her faith, strong in her love of family.

To me, she was the ultimate embodiment of perseverance. She survived greater struggles than most of us have ever known. Angie was born in 1909 in Oliphant Furnace, Pennsylvania, an Appalachian mining town, where her father worked as a coal miner. In 1913, when my grandma was just four years old, she was taken back to Italy after both her mother and one of her younger sisters died suddenly of influenza.

Her father was at a loss for how to care for his three remaining young children, so he got back on a boat to go home to Italy, where his own mother could help him. Unfortunately, by the time he crossed the ocean she too had died. He quickly remarried, a woman my grandmother always described as an especially cruel stepmother, and then went off to war. My grandmother lived with her wicked stepmother, caring for her siblings for several years while my great grandfather was held as a prisoner of war.

Luckily, he survived, and returned home. The evil stepmother gave birth to two more children, and Angie's father went back to working for his cousin, gathering wood on the nearby mountain. My grandmother was educated until the fourth grade and then stayed home to cook, clean, and care for her two younger siblings. They didn't have enough milk to go around, so her stepmother would only give it to her own children. As a result, my grandmother suffered from rickets, which deformed every bone in her body, especially her legs.

After her stepmother became sickly, Angie did most of the housework, cooking, and child-rearing. Can you imagine being ten years old, a bit crippled, not allowed to go to school, treated cruelly, *and* having to take care of two young kids? That's hard. I may face challenges, but my life is nowhere near as hard as that.

Angie's father recognized how harsh life was in Italy and how little opportunity existed for his five children, so he eventually sent Angie's sister and brother to America, but not my grandma. She was the cook, housekeeper, and nanny for her two half-brothers, and her services could not be spared.

Angie remained in Italy for six more years before she finally returned to America in 1931, at the age of twenty-two—just months before her stepmother died and Mussolini closed the borders. Had she stayed any longer, she never would have been able to leave. She came back to an America in the midst of the Great Depression, with unemployment at 16 percent and a banking crisis under way. Speaking no English, she was grateful to find work in a factory, even though she made only 25¢ an hour (the equivalent of $4.25 in today's dollars). It took her eight years of hard labor to pay back her passage. No union benefits. No coffee breaks. She didn't care. She was free. She had a job. The country was free.

Six years later, on the cusp of being an old maid for that day and age, she met another Italian and married my grandfather, Fiore DiLullo. They quickly had two boys, the oldest of whom is my father. Just when things were looking up, my grandfather died suddenly of a ruptured appendix. And there she was, a woman with a fourth-grade education who barely spoke English. A widow, with a one-year-old and three-year-old, at the end of the Great Depression.

She was afraid that if she didn't provide for her children, they would be taken away. So she moved her family into one room of their house and took in boarders. She bought a Singer sewing machine and some clothing patterns, took in sewing and ironing by day, and got a job in a bakery stuffing the jelly into doughnuts at night.

Against all odds, she made ends meet and provided her boys with a comfortable if simple life. My father recounts how delicious her homemade bread was and how proud he was when the nuns at school complimented him on his hand-sewn and neatly pressed clothes. Fast-forward a few decades and both of her boys had gone on to get graduate degrees, far surpassing her fourth-grade education. Her measure of success in life was the well-being and survival of her family.

Angie was never a victim. She called on her strength and spirit to survive.

She didn't use her lack of education or her circumstances as excuses. She focused on what she did have and on what she could do. She was grateful for every day with her sons. She made a choice to be happy. I'm sure she was afraid, but she felt the fear and did it anyway. She was resilient, and she persevered no matter what life threw her way. I am grateful for that inheritance. With a grandma like that, I feel like I come from royalty.

Every single day I am inspired by the resilience of women who, like my grandmother, have been forced to adapt to changing circumstances and have chosen to lead bold and joyful lives despite tragedy. When faced with the choice, they choose less fretting and more doing. Less wanting and more having. They survive. They persevere. And so can you. Whatever you are facing right now, gain some perspective by thinking about my grandmother's generation, who sailed across oceans, fought for the right to vote, went to work when their country went to war, clipped coupons, and raised families. That's some serious perseverance. Whatever your challenges, think about how others before you have encountered far worse. With perseverance, you too can overcome your challenges.

from natural disaster to diamonds

Take Tysh Mefferd's story. When Tysh first became a Stylist with Stella & Dot, she had no idea of where her path would lead. Her perseverance, strength, and belief in herself were rooted not only in her genes but also in her *why*. Her circumstances were unacceptable to her, so she decided to do something about it.

Tysh and her family were under great financial stress in the aftermath of Hurricane Ike. She and her husband, Jon, and their three small children were living in Houston, and its economy had more or less tanked. Tysh had been running a small wedding invitation business out of her home. Jon was a corporate attorney, and they had never worried before about not being able to afford their lifestyle. Yet, with the sudden downturn in the local economy after the natural disaster, her business took a dive and they found themselves in over their heads. Their boys required special occupational therapy, and they were feeling additional financial pressure from a home improvement loan they had signed up for under better times. Tysh knew she needed a plan B.

After jumping on the Stella & Dot website late one night, she thought to herself, *Hmmm . . . if I can sell enough jewelry to earn an* *extra $3,000 a month, that would cover our home improvement loan* and *the occupational therapy for the boys.*

That was her very simple, concrete *why*. Without giving it any more thought than that, she signed up. When she told her husband, he said, "No way! You have way too much on your plate. You cannot do this!" But Tysh was not daunted. She figured she had very little to lose and could at least earn back the under-$1,000 investment she had made. She would make certain of that.

She got busy booking a few trunk shows where she could showcase the product line and earn a commission. After getting the first few trunk shows under her belt and having some early selling success, she headed to a Friday evening show where, even though a few people showed up, she made a big fat zero in sales.

Suddenly all her hopes evaporated. She was overcome with doubt and wanted to quit. The following morning she was supposed to drive to Dallas (over 300 miles away) to attend her first Stella & Dot training event, but now she really didn't think she had it in her.

In tears, she asked Jon what he thought she should do. Surprisingly, he encouraged her to go. His response was, "I know you are disappointed, but I want you to think about something. How many times have you met with bridal clients, spent hours with them, and ultimately they chose another vendor to work with and you made nothing? There is really no difference here. You can't expect a home run every time."

She took her husband's advice. She got up at the crack of dawn, drove five hours, and went to the meeting. There she met other Stylists and Mike Lohner. As Tysh said, "It was *life*-changing. I'm so glad I had not listened to those little voices in my head and instead chose to be grateful for that Saturday morning. I immediately started doing more trunk shows, listening to training calls, and putting into action all the useful tips of what the others who were having success were doing." She didn't overthink it, she just did it.

Fast-forward several months and Tysh from Texas was making thousands of dollars a month, regularly. Yes, she encountered start-up challenges, but she believed in herself beyond measure and believed in her *why* just as much. Today that $3,000 a month goal looks quite small. Tysh has earned well over $3.5 million since she joined six years ago and has broken over $100,000 in a single month. She's earned more than ten all-expense-paid vacations to exotic destinations and has been promoted to our top level, diamond director, and made Stella & Dot history by being the first team to do so. She has done so well that her husband has resigned from his corporate life as an attorney and now works with Tysh from their beach house in Galveston, Texas. With his big Texan charm and huge smile, you have never met a man more eager to admit that his wife was right not to listen to him that first night!

Why is Tysh's story so inspiring? Because she did not expect to have success without doing the work. She did not expect to get rich quick. She kept going even when other people doubted her. She had faith even when her efforts along the way failed or did not have an immediate payback. She invested in herself and her business. She read books and flew to new cities. Sure, she got discouraged and frustrated, as any normal person would, but she chose not to wallow in those feelings for long and got back to the business of succeeding. She always made a point of turning frustration about what was not working into curiosity about how she could do it differently, or longer, to get different results. In the end, it was Tysh's perseverance in spite of obstacles that made her the extraordinary success that she is today.

delayed gratification

Do you remember the Nestlé commercials with the bunny who just couldn't wait to drink up that rich, creamy glass of Quik? Well, studies show that this poor impatient bunny, who couldn't resist the delicious glass of Quik, would not be very likely to do well later in life. When we are young children, one of the most valuable—and challenging—lessons we must learn is how to wait for something. This is a tough thing for humans (and apparently cartoon bunnies). We want what we want *now*! But patience is a virtue, and good things come to those who wait.

Walter Mischel, a psychologist and now a professor at Columbia University, did a series of studies on delayed gratification in the late 1960s and early 1970s, when he was at Stanford. In these studies, a child was offered a choice: having one little treat right now, or waiting and having two treats in fifteen minutes. (This is commonly called the Marshmallow Test, even though the treat used in the study was more often a cookie or a pretzel.) The researchers followed these children to see how they fared later in life. Guess what they figured out? Patience pays. In follow-up studies, the researchers found that the kids who waited the fifteen minutes for the two treats had better life outcomes, as measured by everything from SAT scores to educational attainment, to body mass index (BMI), to other indicators of success and well-being.

Why do you think this is? It's because those who immediately go for the instant reward often end up not developing the tools to figure out how to get more later. As you go down your path, get used to asking yourself with every choice: Is there more value if I wait a bit longer? If I work longer? If I do it a bit differently by developing my skills? If I put in more time? You may have a

Marshmallow Test–like choice in front of you involving an instant reward—perhaps having more free time and money now versus going back to school to switch into the medical field, which you have always been passionate about. Of course, more time and money now seems like the most attractive option in the short term. But what is truly more valuable to you in the long run? A little cash today or the well-paying career of your dreams in a few more years?

I have decided many times to delay instant rewards for the vision of a bigger payoff later. This includes investing every last dime back into our business to expand, as well as putting off business travel in order to get more quality time with my growing kids. Those memories are worth more to me than the so-called instant results of a business trip.

As long as you ask yourself what is worth more in the long run, you might just see that it will pay to be patient. You'll also discover a strong compass for making the right decisions.

you climb a mountain one step at a time

To be extraordinary you don't have to endeavor to set world records; you just have to commit to starting and persevering. You have to believe that ordinary people can do extraordinary things. In fact, they do that every day. They invent cool things. They start successful businesses. They walk across America, climb Half Dome, complete marathons, graduate from college, pay off their mortgages, celebrate five years of sobriety or fifty years of marriage. They profoundly impact the direction of another person's life.

And they do all these things by taking it one step at a time.

When Danielle Redner, our VP of training, turned forty she wanted a big shove out of her comfort zone: she decided to climb Mount Kilimanjaro, the world's highest freestanding mountain. For months she pitched the big idea to friends to get a group to go with her to Tanzania. No takers. "It costs too much to fly to Africa." "It takes too much time to train." "It's too far away." "I'm afraid of heights." "I'm way too out of shape."

After hearing this parade of declines, Danielle accepted that she wasn't going to go with a group of friends, but she knew she could get her husband, Gregg, to go with her. They signed up for a group trip and began to train with a group of "weirdos," as she lovingly referred to them, who would go on to become a group of best friends.

Yet even after going through the training, the morning she woke up at base camp and looked up at the highest mountain on the African continent, she panicked.

As she told me, "At the bottom of the mountain I looked up and said to Siday, my Tanzanian guide, 'How can I climb that?!' He turned to me and said happily, 'Oh, Danielly! You climb a big mountain the same way you climb a small one—one step at a time.'"

At the beginning of the trip, Danielle and her team members were given an emergency card to fill out; it asked them to check off the conditions under which they would want to be airlifted off the mountain. Panic and nausea were options, but the only box that Danielle checked off was "cardiac arrest." As she explained to me, "Don't take me out of the game when it gets hard!"

The lesson? If the option to quit is eliminated, persistence is the default. Just eliminate quitting as an option.

She did panic, and she did get nauseous, but she didn't need the air-vac. Instead of being airlifted off the mountain when the going got tough, she persevered. She made it to the summit. It was the most physically challenging thing she had ever done, and a huge gift to herself. While the views from the top were breathtaking, the best one was her view of just how strong she was.

make it fun, get there faster

One time my family and I were taking a hike. It was a hot, dry California day, and my younger daughter, Tatum, started to complain about an hour in, just beyond the halfway point on our loop. She was hot, hungry, and tired from a sleepover the night before.

She wanted a granola bar, but we were out of granola bars— because she had just eaten the last one five minutes earlier. This was no starving child too weak to continue. She wanted a drink, but was rejecting water. You get the idea. We had arrived in total meltdown town.

Tatum refused to go another step, insisting that she wanted to turn around to get back to the car. Since we were more than halfway home on a loop trail, turning back was the least effective plan of action.

I tried reason. "Tatum, the fastest path back is to just to keep going. You just ate. If you were really thirsty, you would drink the water. It's the best thing for you." All the logic in the world was lost on her.

I tried tough love. "Tatum, there are no shortcuts! Toughen up and get going!"

I even tried to threaten her and guilt her into it. "Come on, Tatum, this isn't fair to the rest of us, we're having a nice family day. Keep this up and you are not going to have sleepovers anymore!"

I tried desperate appeasement. "Okay, honey, Mommy will carry you." It is actually very difficult to hoist up an eight-year-old who is hell-bent on rolling in the dirt.

I don't know what took me so long, but having exhausted all other options, I went with my last-ditch attempt. *Fun.*

"The truth is, Tatum, you are right. We will take a grave risk going beyond this point, but unfortunately we are lost, and we've now wandered right into butt smacker forest. A fierce tribe of half-human creatures lives here. They have hands like gorillas, and they lurk like hidden tigers, crouching behind the trees. When they see humans, they smack them on the butt and scream so loudly that you'll either die of a heart attack or the butt smack.

"You know, it's probably hopeless, but you and I could go ahead, and that way we could try to protect Daddy and Charlie by seeing what might be lurking behind those trees."

Tatum stopped crying and looked at me with a toothy smile and eyes wide with delight. You've never seen a kid sprint so fast, knowing she had essentially been granted permission to jump out from behind a tree and try to whack her sister. Desperate times, desperate measures. But it worked. Why? Because fun works. And it especially works when your destination is farther away than you want it to be and quitting is not an option. Humor works too. Sometimes the only way to persevere is simply to make it fun. Every now and then, we all feel like throwing ourselves in the dirt and having a fit! Instead, you might as well go all in and find the fun that makes all hard situations much, much easier.

the grass is greener where you water it

What area of your life is underwhelming you? Maybe you are not showing up as much as you should in your relationships because you feel like you're in a rut. Or you are frustrated at work and giving only 70 percent of your potential. Or you are staying home with your kids and even though you love them with all your heart, you're constantly struggling inside because you find it a little boring and exhausting to only be around little people all day. You wonder if you should go back to work.

This book is not meant to tell you that you must radically change what you do to be successful and happy. Rather, I want you to make the most of the life you have. Only if you feel it's the wrong one do you need to change it. Perseverance isn't just about accomplishing something new; it's about making the life you have even more extraordinary.

Days, even months, in which you feel less in love with your spouse are no reason for divorce. And days, even months, in which you feel a loss of love for your job is no reason to quit. It is, however, a reason to figure out how to make some real changes so that you can fall back in love and be happy. The happily married parents of a friend of mine shared their secret. An extraordinary marriage is not about the foolish notion that every day you stay madly in love; it's simply the commitment to fall back in love.

Right now, in your life, where do you feel lackluster? What are you doing to fall back in love with your life? What are you doing to fire yourself back up? Maybe you were excited to take the job you're in, but you no longer feel totally passionate about the work. What is it that is missing or different? The people? The project? The leadership style? The process?

Instead of complaining about your job, focus on what you are doing to change it. Instead of stopping at frustrated, shift into curious—about how you can make an impact. Yes, you. You don't need a title or an invitation to make change. You are the change agent, and you are accountable for your own life experience. Not your manager, not HR, not your parents or partner. *You.*

Sticking with something can have great rewards. For example, to get the top position in a company, you may have to stick with it longer than most. Dean Robert Bruner of the Darden School of Business at the University of Virginia reports that while about 17 percent of the business school's graduates change jobs within eighteen months, 41 percent stay at their job five or more years. Moreover, Bruner also notes, those who rise to the *very* top are not job-hoppers at all. They are the ones who stick it out and make the place better. "About two-thirds of all CEOs of the S&P 500 companies were internal appointments, and on average they spent 12.8 years with their company before being appointed."

What if you're not happy in your situation, but it's not about you? What if the problem is really about them? It takes two to tango in all relationships—whether romantic, professional, or social. You may be right—it may be true that others need to step up and pick up the slack. But being right is often different than being effective. Start by asking yourself what *you* are doing to change the relationship versus waiting on others to go first. You don't like the situation? Do something about it.

Be forewarned—extraordinary is also not for the malcontent. By that I mean those who, because they think the grass is always greener somewhere else, cannot be truly passionate about what they have and where they are. Consider the possibility that you are in the right place and you simply need to bring passion into what you've already got. Make your existing choices better. The grass might just be greener where you water it.

help others persevere

One summer I enrolled my then nine-year-old daughter Tatum in a robotics tech day camp. She was so excited when we dropped her off the first day. That is, until they put her into a group with all boys. That night she came home crying and begging not to return the next day. She loved what they were doing in the camp, but the boys either ignored her or threw Legos at her—sometimes hitting her in the face. Of course, the lioness mother in me was ready to go down and put the smackdown on those Lego-throwing #!*&!s. But instead, I just replied, "Tough luck, kid—but you can't let boys make you leave the room." She bucked up and went back. On the last day of camp the battle bots they built competed with each other. And guess what? Her battle bot crushed them all! Forgive my gloating—I can't resist. Some victories are just a little bit sweeter.

But the point of this story isn't just how awesome my kid is (though come on, that's pretty awesome!). The point is that the world is better when we not only persevere ourselves, but when we are thoughtful about the environment we create for others.

The development of world-class talent in science, technology, engineering, and mathematics (STEM) is critical to a country's innovation and global competitiveness. Yet, women are dramatically underrepresented in this area, and the trend is getting worse. Who knows exactly why this is happening? Is it a lack of female role models, gender stereotyping, or less family-friendly flexibility in the STEM fields?

Regardless of the causes, it's clear that men and women alike need to encourage and support women in STEM. What can you do about it? One of two things. One, make sure you don't let boys make you leave the room. And two, don't throw Legos at people because they are different than you. Sometimes, you should go out of your way to help others persevere, too.

stick with the sticky parts

Having a few irons in the fire might make you feel like you are giving yourself options and thus a higher chance of success. But I'm sure you've heard the saying, if you chase two rabbits, they both get away. So be careful about pursuing multiple options, robbing yourself of true focus, and thus preventing your success. When you are working on too many different projects, you can be tempted to shift from one to the other when you encounter something hard or something you don't like. Success requires that you focus and push through. It requires that you commit to the good, the bad, and the ugly. This is true in marriage, in starting a business, and in any role you play at work or in your community. Perseverance means being totally committed to sticking with the sticky parts.

with perseverance, you can run the world

Are you thinking, *This all sounds good, but I am the least likely person to do something extraordinary? I just haven't got it in me!* Well, think again. Let me tell you the unlikely story of Helen and Norm.

Helen was an emergency room nurse who eventually went to

work with her oral surgeon husband, Norman, who was fifteen years her junior. At the age of fifty-five, she retired. At about the same time she retired, Norm was challenged by a friend to run in a ten-mile race.

Helen hated exercise. She had no interest in sports and had been a smoker for twenty-five years. She grew up in a time when girls weren't raised for athletics—they were raised to learn sewing and knitting and how to be a "good wife." She worked, raised their children, and took care of their home. Exercise just wasn't part of her life.

But she didn't want Norm to have to run alone, so she agreed to do it with him. They lived in Kentucky at the time and started training by running around their house. "We ran a fifth of a mile that first day, then added a fifth of a mile each day," she says. After ten weeks, they were running ten miles. "It took me two hours to run the 10-mile race," she recalls. "At the end of the ten miles, I thought I'd never run again." She came in dead last. The only thing she liked about the race was getting to the finish line, because that meant it was over.

She hated running, but Norm didn't. She figured, if she was going to have to go with him to races anyway, she might as well keep running. Soon, though, something changed. The more she ran, the more she wanted to run, and eventually she found she wasn't running for Norm anymore. She was running for herself.

By age sixty-six, Helen had run five 100-mile mountain trail races all over the country—in just a four-month period. At age seventy, she ran a 363-mile, six-day race—that's sixty miles a day for six consecutive days. At eighty-two, she ran the Lake Tahoe Triple—completing a marathon a day for three days in a row at an elevation of over 6,000 feet. Today she's run on every continent except Antarctica. This woman put retiree, ex-smoker, great-grandma, octogenarian, ultrarunner, and Hall of Famer in the same sentence.

At eighty-nine years old, Helen continues to run. And remember, her start was a painful fifth of a mile, after fifty-five years of no exercise. That's perseverance. If Helen can do all that, what can you do?

Helen started running marathons with her legs, but she finished with her head and her heart. You can run life that way, too.

There may be something you want to do but you think you are not meant for it, or you're too old for it, or you're too bad at it. Don't believe it. If you believe and you are willing to persevere, a fifth of a mile at a time, you can run the world.

productivity: dropping the rubber balls

I S THE LAST P REALLY PRODUCTIVITY? WERE YOU HOP-ing for something sexier? Well, productivity *is* sexy, because to love life and get what you deserve, you need to work smarter, not just harder.

People often ask me, "How do you do it all?"

What they really mean is this: how do I manage to be the CEO of a successful group of companies *and* a decent mother and wife who, most of the time, does not appear to be pulling her hair out and neglecting herself? Most people wonder if great parenting, a happy marriage, healthy living, an adventurous life, and a success-ful career can possibly coexist. My answer is a resounding yes.

Now, I promised I would not sugarcoat it. So, was this always the case for me? Was this easy to get to? No and no. Is it possible for you? Is it worth it to try? Yes and yes.

Yes, I have a supportive husband, but I didn't marry that elu-sive magical man who always put my career first and volunteers to do bath and bedtime on his own, right after he makes dinner and right before he gives me a foot rub at the end of each sunshiny day.

Unfortunately, my CEO credentials are not recognized inside my home. It's like a CEO-free zone. My husband and children expect (and deserve) the same wife and mom things of me as any other family.

And you might be thinking, *"Getting the right things done is easy for you to say, sister! You must have a staff of people that do everything for you. Sure you're successful, but you don't have to do the laundry!"* I am well aware that when a successful working mother gives advice, critics are at the ready, on the hunt for privilege, nannies, and neglected children.

Well, I confess, I no longer do *all* of our laundry, but I have that extra support in my daily life *now* because I worked hard in order to afford that, not because I had extra resources all along and that allowed me to be successful. I am not successful because I had resources; I have resources because I created my success. And so can you.

And, like most young families with two working parents, we have child care during the week. But that took a lot of wrangling with guilt and figuring out how we got help with childcare without feeling like we were outsourcing too much of the essential care of our children. In fact, when my youngest daughter, Tatum, was a week old, I took her back to work with me. We were still a very small business, and the concept of maternity leave for most small business owners is simply not a reality.

For me, learning to master my time wasn't easy. Balancing being a young mother while being a start-up CEO was the very hardest part of figuring out how to be happy *and* successful. Growing my business was a piece of cake compared to figuring out how to get it all done in a day in a way that let me live a happy life.

So how did I get there? By saying no, a lot.

I don't do it all. I do what matters most, and so can you. How?

You listen to your own voice telling you what matters. You make trade-offs. And you let go of any guilt about the choices you do make (more on the subject of letting go of your guilt later). Being able to master your life means being able to quiet all the noise that comes with the draining, worthless, false beliefs of inadequacy. When you reclaim the time you used to spend worrying about not doing it all or pleasing everyone, you can repurpose your time and energy toward accomplishing what you need to do to create the extraordinary life you want.

mastering your time

A crucial step to finding your extraordinary is learning the sixth P—productivity—and this requires mastering your time. Why is this so important? Because when you make conscious choices about how you spend your time, treating each hour of your day as if it were precious gold, then you are much more likely to do what matters most to you. You more easily let go of all that is not essential to you and your happiness and have more time to spend on the essentials—the people you love and the activities that yield the highest value.

We all have lots of options and items on our never-ending to-do lists. We all feel like we are juggling balls every day, and we're afraid to drop them. Well, I have good news. Success isn't about not dropping any balls in a juggling act—it is about identifying which balls are rubber and which balls are glass. It's okay to drop the rubber ones—you can pick them back up later. No harm, no foul. But don't drop the ones that are glass.

More good news. Being a master of your own time is not an inherent trait of the lucky few. It's a skill that can be learned through

Balance comes
from identifying
which balls
are rubber and
which balls
are glass.

practice. *Anyone* can go from scattered multitasker to productivity ninja. I admit—I was not always a master of productivity. Yes, I am a recovered time-waster. I did not spend my days watching reality TV and eating bonbons. Rather, I went through my life with the foolish notion that my time was not precious.

During my WeddingChannel.com days, I worked all the time. I was a twenty-four-year-old who had a company full of people to pay. I desperately wanted to create success—for myself and for them—and felt responsible for doing so. I thought *not* working all the time was a disservice to the company. So, for four years, I came in early every morning, ate almost every meal at my desk, and left the office most nights well after 10:00 PM. And yes, that included many weekends. All work and no play, though, not only makes Jane a dull girl, it makes Jane tired, less strategic, and a poor leader.

Of course, starting a company is not a nine-to-five job, and long hours are often required. However, in my case, I didn't even stop working when important tasks were complete. Because I thought working all the time was the only way to signal my commitment to others, I would actually do *lower*-priority items when a request or questions cropped up, knowing I could simply do higher-priority work later. How foolish. How macho!

As I grew older and wiser, I realized that giving your career an endless amount of time creates the dangerous habit of not carefully distinguishing between high-value activities and low-value activities. You simply assume that you should check *everything* off the list, rather than knowing you must always leave unimportant things undone. The problem with this is that if you are ambitious and have imagination, you will always have more on your list than you will complete. You will die with a list.

Luckily, becoming a wife and a mother forced me to refocus on making the most of the limited amount of time I chose to give to my work. It started me thinking about time in terms of mastery, rather than management, which ultimately led me to two big truths about time. These truths now guide my life, as well as how I coach others. Understanding these truths is the starting point of mastering your time and therefore creating the business—and life—you want. After sharing these two truths, I'll offer my five-step process to making the most of your time.

time truths

truth #1: you manage yourself, not time

First, accept that you are in charge of you. You make the choices of what to do with your time, moment by moment, day by day. You do not manage time. Einstein's theory of relativity may state that time is not constant, but I can assure you, for the purposes of maximizing your life, it is. We each get exactly twenty-four hours, seven days of the week. Not even Einstein could change that. But what we *can* change is how we choose to spend those hours.

When people say, "I am just so crazy busy, I can't do it," a more honest statement would be, "I don't choose to do that; it's not my priority right now." If you want to create a life you love, start by eliminating the lie of "I am just too busy." Instead, admit to yourself, "I don't choose that."

Instead of saying, "I just don't have time to exercise!" try, "I chose to sleep from 6:00 to 7:00 AM because I chose to watch TV late last night. I chose the Kardashians over my wellness." Instead of saying, "I don't have time to have dinner with my family," see if this doesn't sound closer to the truth: "I chose to answer twenty more emails instead of leaving the office thirty minutes earlier."

Are these painful admissions? Then change your choices. Do

not keep lying about the scarcity of time. You do not have a monopoly on busy, and if you claim that you do, you are only lying
to yourself, since no one else buys it anyway. The people in your
life intuitively know when you are choosing work over them. Your
body knows when you choose screen time over wellness. Your colleagues know when you choose trivial pursuits over impactful
business activities. Once you acknowledge your power over your
time, "crazy busy" ceases to exist.

Now, this level of honesty might end some casual relationships
earlier than anticipated. Gone would be the excuse, "Oh! I meant
to call, but I have just been so busy." The honest statement sounds
like this: "I did not choose to call you. You did not make the top of
my list." People are never too busy for what they care about most.
You may choose to phrase your choices to others more diplomati-
cally, but still, you have to get honest with yourself about time. You
can't be extraordinary if you have a victim mentality about what
you can't get done because you don't have enough time.

Some people may think their time is taken up by others and it's
not their choice—that their lack of time is somehow unfair. But
time is very fair; in fact, it's one of the fairest things there is. I was
struck by this one day when my youngest daughter was four. We
were throwing a birthday party for her older sister, and she was
complaining.

"Why does Charlie get a party and I don't get one?"

I answered, "Because it's her birthday and not yours. When it's
your birthday in six months, we'll have a party for you!"

"But I want my birthday now! I don't want to wait six months,
that's too much time. It's not fair!" she replied.

"Actually," I responded, "birthdays and time are the fairest
things I can think of. Think about it. Everyone gets just one birthday, and it comes at random. Nobody gets to pick the best one.

People can even have the same one. This is so fair! And time is the same. Everyone gets the same twenty-four hours in a day, seven days in a week, and fifty-two weeks in a year! Big sister or little, boy or girl, rich or poor, old or young—time and birthdays are beautifully fair!"

My four-year-old was not satisfied with this explanation. Her spirits only rose when I assured her that her slice of cake would have a giant icing flower. Nonetheless, if you are over the age of four, it's time to realize that how you spend your time is your choice, not a limiting factor in your accomplishments. Time is *so* fair.

truth #2: you must value your time to have it yield value

It sounds obvious, yet I find that it's an "aha!" realization for many: to create value, you have to do high-value activities. If you want to earn a lot per hour, you have to do things in that hour that yield value the free market is willing to pay more for. If you are doing a task that the free market has determined is worth $12 an hour, you are essentially paying yourself $12 an hour to do it. Do you want to earn more than that? Then you must do something of higher value.

Here is an example: if you have a business and you have ten hours to spend on it a week, should you watch additional training videos so your knowledge can be 100 percent perfect? Go on Facebook and see what other people are doing because it might be useful to you? Or, get on the phone and talk to ten customers? What would you pay someone *else* to do? What would you pay for each activity? Often business owners allocate their time to the least scary activity, or their favorite activity, and avoid the highest-paying activity. They fill their time doing all the low-pay activities and "run out of time" before they do the income-producing activities they would pay someone else more to do. This is not called being busy; this is called procrastination.

If you want to get more value out of your time, shift your time into higher-value activities. Whether you are a business owner, in a corporate job, or trying to get something off the ground as you chase around toddlers, if you don't train yourself to think this way, you may end up spending the majority of your time doing low-value activities. Then you get to the end of the workday exhausted, depleted, and frustrated that you haven't accomplished anything.

Your time will not yield value if you do not value your time!

And you can't just expect to do high-value activities for a short time or just sometimes and create a big payoff. Consistency matters.

Look, if you are happy with what you are getting out of life—in both monetary and other rewards—don't worry about it. But if you want more, you need to look at how you can create and capture more value over an extended period of time.

Here's an example that starts with your hours. You can clean the house, a task you might otherwise have to pay someone $20 an hour to do. But what is your opportunity cost for that hour? Could you do something that paid you more than $20 an hour during that time?

Now let's think longer term. Could you invest an hour to learn something new that may not pay you more than that $20 an hour today but could pay you $50 an hour in the future? Remember, patience pays. You have to be willing to invest in yourself and not expect instant rewards if you ever want to create great value with your time.

This goes back to the bigger question at the heart of becoming

Your time
will not yield value
if you do not value
your time.

extraordinary: what are your life priorities? The first step to time mastery is knowing what you want to accomplish in your career, in your relationship, in anything that's important to you. Now make sure the ways you spend your hours align with your long-term goals.

Without bold questions and a longer-range view, your life can be made up of ordinary actions that feel good in the moment but lead nowhere. You might find that you get to the end of your day or your week and think, *What did I really accomplish?* Those days turn into weeks and months, then years, and ultimately that's your life.

However, when you consciously and consistently identify your purpose and then choose to spend your time in alignment with that goal or set of goals, you make sure that you use your time wisely toward what will make you happy. This is what I think of as living with intention, and it's key to becoming extraordinary.

a talk with yourself about your time

To determine if you are using your time wisely, you need to ask yourself a number of key questions.

What is my long-term goal? What will matter to me in the future? (One year from now, three years from now, etc.?)
Am I spending my time (this week or this month) on the most impactful activities?
Is my energy in the right place to be effective?

I ask myself these questions monthly. When I evaluate my schedule, I don't expect perfection. I just want to raise my awareness and make adjustments so I can get back to a place where I feel right in my life. I often find that these simple reflections are the start of inspiration and action. I not only evaluate my work activities and schedule, I evaluate my work-life balance.

This isn't always easy. Mastering your time includes not only eliminating trivial activities in your life, it includes having to say no to valuable activities, too. You have to understand your limits and set boundaries.

For example, recently I realized my work travel had increased too much. I have always been willing to be a road warrior for the success of the company. I love the personal connection with our field. However, my travel grew as the company grew, and soon I realized I wouldn't just be a road warrior—I was on the verge of being a casualty!

In addition to the travel I do to our regional and various offices in six countries, I travel for our incentive trips and conferences, speaking events and press trips. On top of that, I did field meetings in various cities and I had set a precedent to visit people in their hometown when they are promoted to a very high rank in our career plan.

At times, I would be in three cities in a week and crisscrossing the country several times a month. Often I land after midnight and get up the next day and have a day of back-to-back meetings in order to catch up. I was exhausted, which made me grumpy and less effective. I got sick and lost my voice several times a year.

When I would return home to my family, I'd be a tired husk of a human. I would joke with my children, "Don't go through my pockets for loose change yet! I am not all the way dead—just mostly dead! Go get Miracle Max and I'll be fine." You have to be a *Princess Bride* fan to get that reference.

But the amount I was away was getting to be no joke. I knew it had grown to a point where I would feel regret when my children left the house: they were not always going to be there when I got home from a trip. I knew I had to stop telling myself that my travel was for the good of the company and not under my control. I had to stay true to the fact that I started this company so that I could be in charge of my own schedule, and I have the power to put my family and my health first. After all, I wasn't any good to the company if I came unhinged.

While it is challenging to say no to things that are valuable, the reality is, you can never do it all. Even when I was doing all this travel, it never seemed to satisfy the "need" to do more.

I was trying to do all this in order to not let people down, and yet it was a catch-22—I was letting people down anyway. When I would be in one city, it would just make others wonder why I wasn't in their city, too. I had to be transparent with our leaders and share why I had to change the precedents I had set. Instead of fearing that I would disappoint them, I trusted that they had my back, too.

I had to tap into my belief that our business is much stronger and bigger than me. I had to lose the hero complex that it had to be me or bust doing these trips. I had to get creative and find a way to keep the connection I have with our field, without so many nights away.

If something is swirling in your head and it feels hard, find a way to make it easy. I realized this situation was not really complicated—I made a commitment to my family to reduce my time away from home. I made a hard rule that I would not be away more than an average of five nights per month. Once I established a more reasonable travel schedule as a requirement, it was clear what I had to say no to. I was then able to get creative about other ways to accomplish the same goal of staying connected with our sales field. We added exclusive leadership days and retreats to our existing trips. It may not have been perfect, but I had to accept that it would have to be enough.

Part of me has always suspected that there are too few female CEOs because the demands of the job are more than a woman is willing to take away from her family. There are certainly capable women, but they opt out. I didn't want to opt out of leading my company, so I had to redefine how my role *could* work so that it did not come at too high a cost on my health and my family.

While work travel is a big example, I make these kinds of adjustments frequently on a smaller level. For example, if I realize my husband and I have not had enough quality time together, I make sure we go on a walk or have a date night in the next couple of days. Evaluating how you spend your time will help you redirect, if necessary, on things big and small.

What other hard rule do I recommend? Taking care of *you* is not optional. You can lie to yourself and say, "I have too much work to take the time to eat properly, sleep seven hours most nights, and exercise." Odds are, however, that if you are not taking care of yourself in this way, you are being less than effective and putting yourself at risk of making poor decisions. Taking care of your personal energy is hugely important to getting the most value out of your time.

I love working, and many times I work a bit too much. I get excited about launching a new program and am so inspired that I get wrapped up in the work. I have a tendency to work excessively, so I have to be hyper-vigilant and tune in to when I've reached the point where my work is less than effective. When I am tired, dehydrated, hungry, and restless from no exercise, I get very cranky. Most people do. That's no way to be extraordinary.

I finally got to a point in my career when I realized a few key things. Family time and my personal health are glass balls. Sometimes you *should* stay at work or take a red-eye to cram it in. Sometimes it's okay to skip a family dinner to get work done. But for me, this must be the rare exception, not the rule. Work can't always win, and you can't run yourself ragged trying to catch every ball.

five steps to time mastery

Now that we've gotten a bit more real in how we think about aligning our time with our priorities, here are some practical tips to help you make sure you're getting the most out of your time—so you have more of it to spend on those high-value activities.

1. block your time

Do you often complete your day and think you did not finish enough projects? Time blocking is the antidote. Start by blocking out time for high-value activities. Try to create some big blocks of work time so that you can benefit from the efficiency of focus.

Even if you have kids, even if you work within a large corporation with lots of meetings, you can block out fifteen to twenty minutes on your calendar every morning for a strategic planning meeting with yourself. It will be the most productive meeting of the day. During this time, you will look at your list of priorities and assess which blocks you will use to complete which tasks.

Do things that require more creativity and critical thinking first. The prefrontal cortex is at maximum power first thing in the morning. I don't want to waste that power on the latest email to ding into my inbox or less important meetings. I want to work on what requires the best of my creative energy.

When you are ready to check something important off your to-do list, tackle it with a solid chunk of time. Let's take a simple example to see how time blocking works. Let's assume you have twelve weekly hours to work on a new initiative. That may be four days at three hours each or two hours from 8:00 to 10:00 AM six days a week. Don't amorphously work on it all the time or do an hour here and there, or you're very likely to be inefficient and spend *more* time, never completing the task. The time it takes to complete a task expands to the time allotted.

Here's why. The classic book *The Goal* details a manufacturing principle that is also relevant to personal productivity—switching costs. It's faster and cheaper to run an assembly line for a large quantity of one widget than it is to make a bunch of smaller quantities of a bunch of different types of widgets. That's because switching up the machinery costs time and thus creates a loss in productivity.

The same, it turns out, is true for humans. Every time we start up work or shut it down, it costs us in time and energy, which creates inefficiencies. But it's not just time we're losing—we're also losing brainpower. The part of our brains involved in high-level thinking, the prefrontal cortex, is like a battery. Every time it has to shift from thinking about one thing to another thing—what's called "concept shifting"—the battery is drained a bit. The more our prefrontal cortex is drained, the less capacity we have to think well. So every time you jump from one thing to another, you're reducing your ability to create high value.

Stop checking your phone every three minutes. Nothing that important or interesting has happened. The only thing happening is the scrambling of your thoughts as you self-inflict the dystopia of *Fahrenheit 451*. You cannot expect to get the most out of your life that way.

Research shows that the average worker shifts concepts over 200 times a day, and our constant monitoring of texts, emails, and social media is increasing that figure exponentially. The average time between interruptions is eleven minutes, and it takes most people twenty-five minutes to return to their previous task, if they return at all. The cost? Constant interruptions have been shown to make you distracted, irritable, restless, and frustrated that you are underachieving. Are you convinced now to put your phone away, stop checking email, and avoid switching over to look at Facebook while you are trying to get work done? Put a tracker on your time and have the self-discipline to limit your "rambling" screen time.

You should also block your personal time—drawing a hard line when you need to. For me, I need to block time during the day where I can disconnect—no emails, no texts, no social media, no computer. If you have a family, try making it from 7:00 to 9:00 PM. No-tech time five nights of the week. You'll actually talk to one another! That's what we do—during this period every evening I focus on quality family time, and looking at my phone during that time is considered a grave sin in my household.

Because I have time blocked for both work and family, when I am working I am focused on work, guilt-free. When I am having family time I am focused on that. When I am with my family I let calls go to voice mail. If it's a true emergency, I know they'll keep calling and I'll pick up, but a true emergency is very rare. I've found that separating these two important parts of my life very distinctly is highly effective, for both reducing guilt and getting the most out of whichever activity I'm doing.

2. schedule unscheduled time

You have to know you're pretty regimented when you schedule time to be unregimented. Type A—coming atcha! But alas, that is my secret. I start my day early so I can allow a block of time for unstructured freethinking. Otherwise, I would feel like a prisoner of productivity.

When I create my schedule, I balance tactical, meeting-filled days with one day a week when my schedule is more relaxed and I have time to walk and talk with people in the office. This allows me to address tactical items quickly, without a conference room summit, and to brainstorm new ideas with people. This type of spaciousness in your schedule is crucial for anyone wishing to think more entrepreneurially; without it, you're so focused on the now that you can't see what's coming next or create something new.

I also try to work from home a couple of Fridays a month. On those days, with fewer meetings and less interruptions, I give myself more space and flexibility so that my brain is not constantly engaged in day-to-day problems. This allows me to think about more strategic, long-term, and future-oriented business issues—issues that have high value for me.

3. assess your time: track it and review it

I am a big fan of time tracking, not because I think we should be slaves to productivity—that would make most of us miserable—but because I want to make sure I am generally doing what I set out to do. Just as you might track what you eat or how often you exercise, tracking how you spend your time helps you get a realistic picture of where your hours are actually going. Research shows that people who track time are more effective at meeting their goals, whatever they may be, because tracking heightens their awareness and they can make adjustments as needed. I suggest that you schedule an hour or so with yourself monthly to assess your time. Your assessment doesn't need to be scientific. Just look over what you've done for the past several weeks.

When you evaluate how you've spent your time, don't be overly critical. Never think that there's some Nirvana where every minute of your day is optimized and you only do things that serve your life's calling or for which you have a comparative advantage. That would be misery-making. Who cares how productive you are if you are unhappy? That is no way to live. Everything in moderation—including moderation! Instead of aiming for perfection, think: *Am I generally doing things that will take me where I want to go?*

Identify your time traps—those activities that are bringing you little or no value or happiness. We all have guilty pleasures—that's fine. Just evaluate how much time you are spending on your guilty pleasures and decide if they are getting in the way of your other priorities. In fact, if you are doing plenty of what serves you with the rest of your time, go ahead and strike the word *guilty* and simply see those activities as pure pleasures!

4. get real with your schedule

I'm a working mom. I have a full-time, successful career, and here is what I do each week:

- I cook a healthy dinner each night—with only locally sourced organic foods.
- I leave work early to pick up each child for a special mommy-daughter date.
- I mostly work from home.
- I dote upon my husband, leaving love notes in his sock drawer.
- I study Italian.
- I train for a triathlon.

- I take pride in my appearance—looking fashionable is a way of expressing my confidence.

Just kidding! Here's what is going on in my *real* life:

- I cook ahead on Sundays and make three meals at a time. My children are very sick of my chili, but it's healthy and it works.
- I am at my kids' school *maybe* a few times a month. We have special time on the weekends, which I have to beg them for, because they'd rather play with their friends anyway.
- I work from home all right. I get in at least several hours of work on the weekend and often work after the kids go to bed during the week. But I also go into the office from about 9:00 AM to 6:00 PM during the week. And everyone is still alive, with no need for therapy.
- I *own* Rosetta Stone Italian, but it's still in the box.
- I choose exercise over primping. People can tell when I have to film something at work because it looks like I actually blow-dried my hair.

In other words, I do a lot every day, every week, but I don't do it all. I do only what matters, and what I love. And I don't regret it or feel guilty about it either. Why? Regret and guilt are among the most futile of emotions—and a terrible waste of time.

5. don't let other people hijack your time and priorities

Most people let others consume their time. They accept every calendar request and conference call—and as a result, they are very busy and yet completely unproductive, accomplishing no high-value tasks. Do not disavow your personal power by letting requests from others be a master puppeteer of your life. Don't tell yourself for a second that you do not control what meetings you sit in or activities you sign up for. If you feel they are unproductive or unsatisfying, find a solution. Do not let others hijack your time and priorities.

In a world where you are always connected, you need to be responsible for keeping your life in check. Turn off your phone. Don't get upset if someone is sending you emails at 10:00 PM, but don't feel like you must respond to them. You can't expect to be able to work on your time if you get upset when someone works on his or hers.

At our corporate offices, we try to hire self-driven people. We need people who are capable of managing their own work-life sanity. I tell them, "You have to protect your own work-life balance. People don't have bad intentions, but they will use your time however you let them. Take control of the situation and set boundaries."

I once forgot what coast an employee was on and called her at 6:00 PM her time, right as she was picking up her daughter from day care. She missed the call, then called me back right away and apologized profusely. Realizing the time, I replied, "Actually, don't apologize to me! Apologize to yourself for apologizing to me!" You should feel very strong and confident for (a) not answering, or (b) saying, "It's school pickup time for me, so this is a bad time to talk. If this is urgent, I can talk after she goes to bed, but if not, can we chat in the morning?"

Additionally, no matter what your title is, be responsible for how effectively your time—and other people's—is spent during your workday. Don't set meetings for sixty minutes when you need thirty. Don't invite twenty people to a meeting when you need five. Make sure that all meetings have clear agendas and you move to a resolution. Don't sit in meetings in which you are not contributing. If others are scheduling and running meetings this way, be sure you give them constructive feedback. Yes, you can do that.

Do you feel guilty skulking out of the office to attend your kid's Tuesday afternoon sports game? If you sometimes work during the evening and weekend, you should stand tall when you sometimes want to be there for your family during work time.

Always get your work done well, and always be your best, but remember that *you* control you. Others will control your time if you let them. Don't let it happen.

bonus tip: make *yourself* a priority

I'm sure that, as astute readers, you have come to the conclusion that underlying all of this advice on how to master your time is one simple truth: You absolutely must take care of yourself if you want to be happy. If you want balance. If you want success. If you want extraordinary.

A friend of mine once told me he looks at time spent on vacation in Hawaii as bonus time since he figures those days are getting added back to his life with all the de-stressing he is doing there. I feel that way about my daily exercise and healthy eating.

You don't have to be able to jet off to Hawaii to relax. You've got two feet and a front door. I rarely decide that I do not have time to go for a thirty-minute run on a busy day. I believe that a thirty-minute run or forty-five-minute exercise class gives me hours of higher-quality energy later, so it's like I'm saving time. Exercising is how I chill, and it is when I am most creative. Some of my best ideas have come while I'm running. (I got the idea for

WeddingChannel.com when I was on a treadmill!) I don't have time *not* to run.

Taking care of you is hugely important to maintaining all those balls in the air and getting close to that balance we are all trying to achieve. In order to be strong-minded, I need to feel strong in my body. I need that energy to manage all my priorities and to get it all done. I am convinced that I'd accomplish less than half of what I do if I did not make my physical well-being a priority. Exercise calms me, clears my head, and makes me more focused, helping me work more efficiently. It also helps me sleep better at night. Once, a woman said to me, "It's amazing that you fit exercise into your daily routine, I just do not have that hour in my day!" I might have been a bit harsh—I turned to her and said, "But you do. You have a 5:00 AM in your day too." I want to be honest about what it takes and why it's worth it.

I love having a day loaded up with activities. Sure, I like to unwind and vacation, but in general, I love having a packed schedule and checking things off the list. My sister recently said to me, "You relax by doing. Other people relax by, well, relaxing." It's true: I naturally prefer a bustling pace, so it's not brave or hard for me.

All people deserve to put their health and wellness first. Parents who are often busy and sleep-deprived need to take care of themselves. Busy executives who are trying to balance an intense career with their life need to take care of themselves. Do you really believe the needs of others have to come first during all twenty-four hours of your day?

Consider this: Making your health a priority is not being selfish at all. It's about being the best version of yourself that you can be, so you can bring that extraordinary you to your work, your friends, and your family. The people you are working with and taking care of are much better off with a better you!

invest in yourself

After you've cleared your schedule of things that don't make your heart sing, you have time to invest in yourself and learn something new. I am a voracious reader, with a pile of books and magazines by my bedside. I may not read them all cover to cover, but I am naturally curious and feel happier when I am discovering something new.

When was the last time you stretched your brain? Felt uncomfortable as a beginner? Your brain is game for it, if you are. Our brains can grow new neurons and neural cells (a process called neurogenesis), which means they are always ripe for learning.

Consider yourself a student for life. How do you want to grow? Think of how Cindy started a business. Think of Danielle and her drumming. Think of Helen and her marathons. Think of you! Here are some things to consider:

Stack up some books in topics that interest you (Find a list of my current reads at www.helloextraordinary.com)
Take a course
Attend an industry conference
Reach out to those with a shared interest and ask to connect

Extraordinary You

- If you don't choose something, don't trick yourself into thinking you're too busy. You're not too busy. You're choosing not to do it.
- Get clear on your high-value activities, both personal and professional.

- Time-block your schedule and track how you're doing.
- Want more help mastering your time? Find book recommendations and more tips at www.helloextraordinary.com.
- Make it a priority to continually invest in both your health and the process of learning and discovery.

part three

The Best Version of You

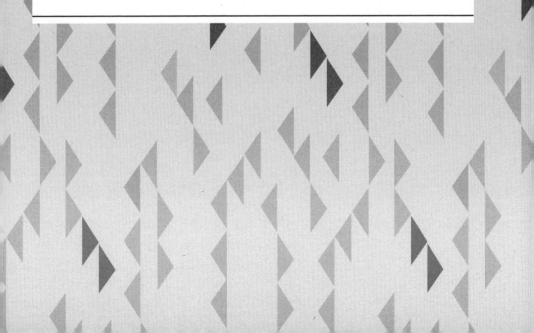

gratitude

It's not happiness that brings us gratitude. It's gratitude that brings us happiness.

I KNOW—IT SOUNDS SO TRITE! SO PREACHY. BUT GRATItude is where it's at. Learn to look at the world through the lens of what you have rather than what you don't have. If you are grateful, you always have enough. If you focus on what you don't have, you will always have it tough. Make it a practice to be grateful, *out loud*, every day.

When my children whine or complain for no good reason, I ignore their gripes and just ask them what they are grateful for. No doubt, they find this super-annoying. I find it annoying when I do it to myself! But it *works*. It's hard to moan and groan about how unfair life is when you switch your mind to how fundamentally lucky you are. I do this all the time.

Remember the mini mental vacays I mentioned earlier? A key component of these is a one-minute reflection on what I am grateful for. The vision of my daughter's freckles, for example, never gets old. I could think about that three times, every day, for the rest of my life.

When I'm feeling sorry for myself, maybe I'm trying to resolve a conflict between people or we're not getting the results we hoped for from a big effort, I pull myself back together with thoughts of gratitude to restore my perspective like, "How lucky am I? My worst-case scenario in this situation is still fine. My kids are healthy; I have a wonderful family, and a life I love." It's not that I don't care about resolving the situation; it's just that I am better equipped to move forward when I am calm, and gratitude helps to restore my peace of mind.

It's easy to take what you have for granted. You forget to think about all that you have since it's your everyday. Gratitude is something that takes work to keep top of mind. But sometimes there are experiences or moments when it hits you over the head how grateful you are to have what you have. Let me tell you about one of those moments for me.

In 2011 our Stella & Dot Foundation partnered with buildOn to build two schools in Nicaragua. Chad and I, along with a few Stylists, traveled to a small mountain village just north of Managua to join the construction crew.

Though the miles were short, the journey was long and bumpy in the old school bus we rode over the unpaved roads.

When we arrived, we saw a beautiful town, but with a shocking level of poverty. The family we stayed with was made up of three young moms, living together with their young kids. Nine people were living in one "room," though it was tough to call it a room given that it had no floor and the rickety walls were made of scrap wood.

There was no electricity, no running water, no floor, and no dads. The men were off in Costa Rica, where they could get work and send home some money. The only grown male we encountered was a boy who looked about sixteen; one little girl called him *el otra papa* (the other father).

Each morning we had beans and rice. Each afternoon, beans and rice. Each evening, beans and rice. A few days in, our jokes were all about beans and rice. "Hey, want to meet up after work and maybe grab some beans and rice?" "What do you want to do for lunch? I have a hankering for beans and rice."

Then, we heard someone in the village had eggs. Our American crew was beyond excited at the possibility. Everyone around the table perked up and started inquiring, "Eggs! Where can I get an egg? We have eggs?" It was all we could talk about that afternoon on the job site. It would be so amazing to just have *one* egg.

By evening, after a hard day of labor, Chad and I would be in our sleeping bags, ready to sleep, but we'd inevitably be interrupted by the family's prized pig wandering through our area, along with a stray dog and some other wayward animals. (The pig was not a pet. The family was excited that they'd eventually eat him.)

The sun would rise at 5:30 AM, and all the kids would already be up, doing their chores. Sweeping the dirt, feeding the pig, gathering firewood, all smiling and laughing. Not once did we hear a complaint escape their lips. They were just grateful they had one another, and rice and beans. They only had one plastic chair, so they would take turns sitting to eat.

As we dozed off at night, we would just hear laughing. When we woke up, we would hear laughing. On the construction site, the kids would run around us playing games as though they didn't have a care in the world.

They had almost nothing, but they found deep joy in everything. You could see how grateful they were for what they had.

I have never been more amazed at the power of gratitude.

Though the eggs never materialized, a more important life lesson did. In my daily life, even on my worst days, one or two dozen eggs sit in my refrigerator—inside my house that has a sturdy floor and walls. When I need to cheer myself up, I just shout "EGGS! We have eggs!" When my children are complaining—all I have to do is give them the stink-eye and they say, "I know, I know—we have eggs."

When was the last time you looked in your fridge and marveled at your eggs? Don't you see—you *do* have so much to be grateful for.

After a gratitude reflection it's hard to follow the thought with "Ugh! Now I have to go to work." Instead think "Wow, I am so lucky to live in a country with an economy that provides *a* job for me." Not everyone, even in America, is so fortunate.

The story of my grandma Angie that you read in chapter 7 is similar in many ways. She too had so little, and yet she found a way to be grateful for so much. *I'm* grateful for all that she endured so that I can be here now. Compared to hers, my life is an embarrassment of riches. What could I possibly have to complain about?

what i learned from going undercover

I have a confession: I believe in karma. I believe so strongly in the power of gratitude that I believe that when people do good things for others, they create positive energy that comes back to them. Essentially I see gratitude as a gift you send out into the universe that one day will come back to you in the form of love, joy, and more gratitude.

When I was first approached about appearing on the hit show *Undercover Boss,* I thought, *No way on earth am I doing that!* I tend to think of "reality" shows as people throwing boxed wine into other people's faces, which, luckily, has nothing to do with my reality. I had never seen the show and didn't think I wanted anything to do with it.

Yet when the producers shared the premise of the show with me—to surprise deserving employees with life-changing rewards—I was intrigued. I watched one episode with my family so we could check it out. We were all crying happy tears by the end. Okay, this was different. I loved the idea of doing something really over the top for our deserving employees. At Stella & Dot, recognition is a huge part of our culture. We do a lot of it: lavish our independent sales field with trips, trophies, award galas, dance parties—all very well deserved. But appearing on *Undercover Boss* was an opportunity to celebrate and recognize the people who worked for our home offices, which are situated around the country. While these employees get a fixed salary that our commission-only sales field does not, we have many unsung heroes in our company who don't get to partake in the trips and trophies and who deserve to be celebrated.

There is no doubt that our brands would not be what they are without our different product teams that make top-notch product—from the science team that formulates breakthrough skincare, to the New York–based design team that creates irresistible fashion jewelry, to the technology team that makes our products easy to sell through mobile and social media. At the end of the day, though, if no one ships out that box, everything that happened up to that point is irrelevant, isn't it? The jobs in our distribution center may be less glamorous, but they are no less important to our success.

Filming the show was an opportunity to celebrate the extraordinary people working at our first distribution center in Groveport, Ohio. I was going in as my alter ego, Nicole, a contestant on a decoy reality show. Though my blond wig, heavy makeup, dark contact lenses, glasses, fake nails, mouthpiece, and bedazzled outfit were a pretty good disguise, I was afraid I was going to be discovered at any moment. I didn't think I would stay undercover, but I was confident that my day there would not reveal some kind of disaster scenario with the way our company was run. I've always been very proud of the amazing team running our distribution center. Our mission is painted on the wall.

To give every woman the means to style her own life.

But our people-focused management team did more than just deliver on that mission—they made Stella & Dot a great place to work for those who helped us fulfill that mission every day.

When I arrived, I was introduced to a young man named Tyler, a twenty-three-year-old with a buzz cut and an infectious smile. The ruse was that he was going to try to teach me his job and then make a recommendation to the judges on whether I was a person worth giving money to to start a business.

As we did our job, I got to know Tyler well. I asked him where he grew up and about his family. He'd grown up poor, with a single mother and a brother who both struggled with addiction. Tyler was an open book. He told me about what a great guy his brother was when he was sober and how much he wanted to help him. He talked about how his mother did her best in spite of her struggles, and how much he loved her. This young man was filled with gratitude.

I also asked about his history with the company, what he thought of his job, and what he saw himself doing in the future. He talked about how he had been there since day one. He was so proud of that! Since day one, when it was a construction site with a port-a-potty outside in the middle of the Ohio winter, Tyler had shown up every day, with a smile, doing every job possible. It was a tough start, but Tyler was just happy for the work; he had been

unemployed for months and was sleeping in his car or couch surf-
ing to get by.

When it came to his future, he wasn't sure where he was
headed. He thought he might want to be a dental hygienist. When
I asked him if he had a passion for clean teeth, he said no—he just
was figuring out what the cheapest way was to get any kind of degree that would pay him more. He never entertained the idea that
one day he could have a job that was both secure and something he
really enjoyed. A career where he could be extraordinary. Though
he did not yet have a vision for his future, I knew he would find
and follow his passion, because he had deep gratitude and gener-
osity in his heart.

Next, he told me this story. When our new shipping center
opened up just before the holiday season of 2013, our team was
kicking into high gear, with many of our crew opting for overtime and putting in long days on their feet. We shipped well over
10,000 orders each day. Tyler was one of the hardest workers from
the start, so he knew how it felt to stand on your feet all day. Tyler
took his paycheck and went to Walgreens to get shoe inserts to
ease the strain on his weary feet. Only he didn't get just one pair.
He bought shoe inserts for over 100 people and handed them out
as gifts to his coworkers. Tyler had so little, yet as soon as he had
something to share, he thought about what he could do to help
make others a bit more comfortable.

No surprise that as Tyler's story unfolded during the show,
millions of Americans fell in love with this charming young man
with a heart of gold.

But he didn't go out of his way to be extraordinary just when
the cameras were rolling. At the end of the day, after filming, I
was whisked away into a dressing room RV in the parking lot so
that I could take off the itchy wig without having my cover blown.

Be someone
another person
is grateful to have
in their world.

As I looked out the window, I saw a beat-up car leaving our distribution center parking lot, and I could see it was Tyler behind the wheel. As he was pulling out, someone was approaching the curb in front of him but wasn't yet close to the crosswalk. Tyler stopped anyway, rolled down his window, and said a cheery, "Hello! How you doing?" with a giant smile. He waved the guy across—and you could see this random stranger just light up from this unexpected kindness.

Tyler is the kind of guy who does the kind thing when no one is looking. He didn't buy people shoe inserts because he wanted to be a hero—he simply wanted his hardworking colleagues to be more comfortable. He embodies the spirit of gratitude and kindness, and it seemed that the world was about to take notice.

I was more excited than ever about the secret I knew was coming. In just a few days we were going to give Tyler money to pursue an education that he was really passionate about. That's what I mean by karma: Tyler had always acted with a grateful heart, and now the world had begun to show up for him. To me, Tyler's story shows the power of how you ultimately attract who you are and get what you deserve. So be kind; be grateful, and most of all be someone another person is grateful to have in their life.

every day is a gift

At the end of the day, we all have one very basic thing to be grateful for. Life. Every day aboveground is a good one. Here's how one person learned to take on that perspective.

One day, on the streets of San Francisco, a down-and-out man who was trying to put his life together was walking to a methadone treatment center. At that same moment, a young woman was running an errand for work. She stepped into the crosswalk, and at that same moment an eighteen-wheeler with no side-view mirror gunned the engine and made a right turn.

The woman was dragged forty feet until the homeless recovering drug addict ran close enough to the driver that he got the driver's attention and stopped him.

The homeless man ran to the woman's side—was she even alive? He bent down closely and couldn't tell if she was breathing. "Hold on, I am going to get help," he whispered to her.

The man stood up without a clue of what to do. A passerby ran into a shop to call an ambulance. Then the recovering drug addict looked down the sloping street and saw a giant, sturdy Caltrans front-loader. Having once worked in construction, he recognized this powerful machine and ran toward it. He hopped up into the cab and noticed that the keys were inside.

Then, in the middle of one of the busiest streets in San Francisco, he turned the front-loader around and headed back to the site of the accident. Maneuvering the loader under the eighteen-wheeler, he lifted the truck and freed the woman from its clutches just as the ambulance arrived.

The woman had suffered a fractured sacrum and nerve damage in her spinal cord. She was told that she would never run or ski again and that her body was so traumatized that her ability to have children was questionable.

Following the accident, she spent many long months in a hospital, battling pain and the anxiety of physical and emotional recovery. Her muscles and nerve endings were raw and untethered. She was weak and in constant, relentless pain. Yet instead of focusing on her pain or the future challenges that had been thrust upon her in an instant, she focused on her goal: to get back to living.

After two and a half years of rehabilitation, which was its own form of hell on earth, the woman got back to living. Leaning on the tremendous support of friends and family, she never gave up.

But the story doesn't end there. Turns out, the former drug addict—now hero—stayed in touch with the woman. Throughout her long recovery, they spoke regularly, and soon she became *his* inspiration to recover—to quit drugs and get his life together.

So this is a story of two lives saved. Just as he saved her, so, too, did she save him. How's that for karma?

The woman in this story is none other than my business partner and the co-creator of the Stella & Dot Family of Brands— Blythe (Henwood) Harris. So you see, her story is not just one about passion, but one about unbelievable perseverance and gratitude as well.

Her story is extraordinary, and not just because of the unbelievable timing—a front-loader being there in the middle of a busy city street with the keys in it—and the unlikely hero appearing at just the right moment to save her from the clutches of the 18-wheeler. More important, her story is extraordinary because her courage, her tenacity, and her commitment to her own life led to a recovery no doctor thought possible.

Since that time, twenty years ago, Blythe has gone telemarking in the Alps, ridden elephants in India, and gone rock-climbing in Thailand. When she's not in our design studio in New York, she is often running in the foothills of Marin County. When we decided to green-light the idea for our new company, KEEP Collective, we were paddleboarding in the ocean together. Most remarkable of all, her body, despite back pain and a glued-back-together pelvic bone, brought two utterly perfect and amazing children into the world. Of course, her husband had a little something to do with it, but it was Blythe's spirit and body that defied all the odds.

Blythe has true grit, but most of all she has gratitude that she gets to spend another day in this world. She continues to live boldly, believing that every moment of her life after that day is all gravy. It's as if she lives like any minute she might just get run over by a bus. (Don't worry—she also has a great sense of humor, and that's one of her favorite jokes!)

Any day alive is a good one.

my own gratitude

My story is partly the sum of the stories of all the people who have been a part of my life.

When I am backstage at our national sales conference, I am always overwhelmed with gratitude. Right before we begin we have a parade of the top achievers. I can't wait to see these friends, old and new, with heads held high as they line up to strut across the stage to thunderous applause.

These moments when I witness the accomplishments of others are so joyous that I can barely contain my emotion. Many of our independent business owners are like family to me. We've been through so much together—we've traveled together, laughed together, been to one another's homes, seen one another's kids grow, and watched one another grow.

I know about all the different *whys* of each individual there. One woman was struggling to get pregnant, and now, thanks to her hard work, she can afford the fertility treatments. Her husband is deployed, and the new friends she's met in our community surround her when she needs support. Another woman is paying for her kid's tuition and is no longer in debt. Being back at work—earning real income and achieving the confidence that comes with this level of success—has given her back her mojo after she'd been feeling a bit lost in motherhood. Yet another woman is happier than she's ever been before now that she quit the job she hated.

Their paths have not been all smooth. There were tears of doubt along the way. Some weren't sure they could make it all work. Yet they all persevered.

All of these women bring so much *real* life into the room, so much energy as well as the promise that success is always possible if you work hard enough for it. As it says in our manifesto, passion and joy are a woman's best accessories. And, in that moment, it could not be more clear that it's the strength in women that makes them beautiful.

It's the strength in women that makes them beautiful.

Why am I so grateful? When I see these women I think just one thing: *impact*. The impact that our mission has had on this group of people, the impact that they have made on their own lives, and the impact that this community has had on me. It's what I was looking for all along. That's why I have found my extraordinary. And I hope that something I've learned along my journey will help you find yours.

CHAPTER 10

one tribe

> The most fulfilled women . . . are those who produce their work the way our evolutionary model suggests . . . in flexible, family-friendly environments, in which the work hours can wrap around the ebbs and flows of the dramas of parenting, and in which a strong, respected community of other women understands these seemingly disparate forms of accomplishment and cheer each other on.
>
> —NAOMI WOLF

FOR ME, GIVING UP GUILT WAS A CRITICAL STEP IN my journey to finding extraordinary. In fact, I could never have really been happy if I hadn't figured out that I had to be okay not pleasing all the people all the time. This lesson took me quite a while to learn, and it really began when I had to worry about more than just me in the world. I have always thought as a single person you can prioritize yourself (your education, your adventures, etc.), then as a couple you need to equally care for someone else, and *then*, when you become a parent, the kids come first. Though women physically have children, truly our children have *us*.

Just a year after graduation, I went back to my college campus to recruit engineers to join Trilogy, the company I was working for in Texas. It was at the engineering recruiting barbecue that I met my future husband for the first time. About six months later, Chad had joined the company. A few weeks in, we started dating.

Within a few more weeks, we both knew we'd get married. Four years later, we did, and we haven't looked back since. Chad has always been my rock and is the best thing that has ever happened in my life. Since the day we met, my feet have simply been more firmly planted on the ground. My love for him made me, for the first time in my life, want to focus on something other than just my education or career. I wanted to focus on our family too, because nothing made me happier. Suddenly, my prized independence was a lot less interesting than our togetherness.

When Chad and I got married, I was starting a company (the early version of WeddingChannel.com). He knew I loved to work, and he knew he was marrying someone who did not plan to stop working after having kids. Even though we both went into our marriage with this expectation, that didn't stop me from experiencing the guilt of a working mom when we actually had kids.

Where did this guilt come from? Well, I'm sure my traditional heritage had something to do with it. After Chad and I were married, I remember my Italian grandmother saying to me: "What's the matter with you? You got a husband! Why you working? Why no kids? Oh madone de mia! You keep traveling, you gonna get pregnant—you not even know who the father!"

This last comment has always amused me.

By this time, my grandmother was in her eighties and watching too many daytime talk shows with paternity test reveals. Despite her dramatic form of expression, the message was still sent and received. What on earth is a married woman doing traveling away from her husband and working versus staying home and having kids?

Actually, I didn't altogether disagree with her. I *did* want a family. I *did* miss my husband when I traveled for work. At the time, WeddingChannel.com was based in Southern California, but Chad was going to graduate school at Stanford in Northern California, so I was commuting from San Francisco to Los Angeles on a weekly basis.

Four years after we got married, our first daughter, Charlotte, was born. Even though we both were going to continue working, we agreed that hands-on parenting would always come before *our* careers. But there was an unspoken traditional expectation within that agreement—the kids would come before *my* career. It wasn't just our desire; I told myself it was the expectation of society at large—and that led to a lot of self-inflicted guilt.

On some level, I thought my wanting to work after becoming a mother qualified me as a bad mom and wife. And what about not just wanting to work, but taking on starting a company, which is like work on steroids?

After we moved back to California from Texas, I was bootstrapping Stella & Dot with the proceeds of the sale of WeddingChannel .com, which meant I was not paying myself. Even though we had worked hard to get our savings to a place where we could comfortably get by without my income, I still felt bad about *not* earning money. And, I felt bad for working, period. So you see, my guilt was double-edged and actually made no sense at all. That is one of my points here: most women's guilt makes absolutely no sense, mine included.

Because I felt like my work was a guilty pleasure that I should somehow apologize for, I tried to do *everything* for our family and didn't ask my husband to do more because he was the one who had the "real" job. A couple of years later, after our second daughter, Tatum, was born, when she would get up in the middle of the night, so would I, 100 percent of the time. If our kids needed to go to the doctor, I took them, 100 percent of the time. It wasn't that Chad pressured me to do all the child care; I simply believed that this was what was expected of me—by Chad, by his family, by my family, and by the rest of the world!

I was working full-time and still felt pressured to be the perfect homemaker. If other moms were planning an elaborate birthday party, I felt I had to do the same for my kids. When it came to putting food on the table, I believed not only that I had to cook my family dinner every night, but that I had to pin recipes and make elaborate meals or I was less of a wife.

For the first few years of parenthood and the beginning of Stella & Dot, I kept up the superwoman act. Every day when I got home from eight hours at work, I would play with the kids and then be ready to greet my husband with a kiss when he got home. I would make us dinner, bathe the girls and get them to bed, then get back on my computer and keep working, since the work I had to do to build a company from scratch did not fit neatly into 8:45–4:45.

Ultimately this Stepford Wife act reached a breaking point. While on a family vacation in San Diego, I asked my husband to fly home with our two-year-old and four-year-old so that I could stay and do a two-hour work meeting and then go home on a later flight. I was so excited: we had a high-potential leader in the area, and she had invited me to her home to meet and train a group of potential Stylists.

Chad said he had a much more "reasonable" solution. He would fly home alone, and I would take the kids with me to my work meeting. Then I would fly home with them later. Seriously, that was his idea, and one he insisted on for days. "It's too hard for me to fly home with them alone. But you can do it. Honestly, you can handle anything."

That was my grand "aha" moment: it suddenly became crystal clear exactly where my superwoman act had landed me. I was trying to live up to what I thought my grandmother expected a "good wife" would do, as well as be everything my own mother wasn't, all while trying to be the entrepreneur I wanted to be—without letting anyone see me sweat. And had I really taken the nicest man in the world and created a monster?

It was time to renegotiate the contract I had put in place with my own family.

how i gave up guilt

Luckily, after I essentially hit the ceiling over his San Diego suggestion, Chad was more than willing to take a new look at how we divided up our parental duties. But first, I had to clearly communicate what help I needed if we were to balance both of our ambitious careers and if I was to let go of the pursuit of perfection. "Good enough" was going to be the new "great." Things had to change before I died alone on "I Can Do It All!" Island.

"This is your official notice. Your level of service is being downgraded," I announced to my husband. I went on to explain that this downgrade in service was really great news for him, because I didn't really like the perfect supermom very much and she was making me miserable. Given that he wanted me to be happy, we were going to have to ditch her. And so we did.

I saw that something had to give. I had to start asking people for more help, and I had to stop feeling inadequate all the time. I needed to simplify what I was doing to focus on what mattered most to our family and stop worrying about what people would say . . . or not say.

I had to stop thinking my success as a wife and mother was inversely correlated to the hours I worked and positively correlated to how many meals I prepared for my family, how tidy my house was, and how much I doted on my husband. I had to stop thinking that if I wanted our kids to be with a parent every single day at 5:00 PM sharp, that parent always had to be me. In short, I needed to ditch the guilt.

And eventually I did. I stopped thinking that being a woman who *loved* to work made me any less of a great mother and wife. I can now look back to that breaking point in San Diego as a huge gift. It helped me snap out of my guilt and get my life back under control.

I gave up being perfect, but I never gave up on being extraordinary. I am still a mom working—the mom part comes first. I spend both high-quantity *and* high-quality time with my family. And if there is anything I am most proud of and feel the most confident in, it's that I am just the right mother for our two girls. It doesn't matter to me if anyone other than Charlie and Tatum—and their daddy—thinks so. They are the only three people who get a vote.

As a working mom, I can clearly see all the ways in which my children have benefited from literally being born into my business. As they've grown, they've sat and read next to me while I'm having conference calls. They both have tremendous business acumen for their age and a fierce work ethic. I'm proud of that. And all the time, they tell me how proud they are of me. To me, no one's opinion matters more.

Chad goes from zero to hero in this story. He is now the most supportive husband imaginable. He changed his job to one that required no global travel. He leaned in even more at home. And at this point in our life he takes the lead on the kids' schedules and is an extraordinary dad, all while he balances a challenging career as a tech investor. He lives with three ladies who adore him. It didn't happen overnight, but we got to a place where our family runs the way *we* want it to, regardless of the expectations of others.

When we got married, during our wedding ceremony the reverend said that marriage is a partnership in which each partner is meant to take the other's burdens and make them half, and take each other's joys and make them double. When I gave up the Stepford Wife act, that kind of partnership could finally come true for Chad and me.

How was I finally able to give up the guilt? It happened when I listened to my own heart with enough confidence to know that I was only trying to please a very small list of people, and I was on that list, too. How was I able to find joy instead? It happened when I was able to say to my husband, "This is what my joy looks like. Now let's start doubling it!" And he has done his part—every day since. And I do the same for him.

Remember: no one can have it all, or do it all. Who would want to anyway? Being extraordinary isn't about doing it all; it's about doing what truly matters to you—guilt-free. Only when you give up the guilt can you finally find your true path to success, to happiness, to extraordinary. It's like landing on the moon: one huge step for womankind.

it's time to get happy on the rise

About a year before I began writing this book, the *New York Times* published a cover story on the divergent paths of the Stanford class of 1994. The headline read, "A Gender Gap More Powerful Than the Internet," and I was featured in a photo captioned, "Jessica DiLullo Herrin, an exception."

This should have been a pinch-me moment. I was on the cover of the *New York Times,* pictured with my daughter at a football tailgate party during my twentieth college reunion. I was being called out for being one of the only females from my class who had succeeded as a tech entrepreneur.

At first glance, I loved the article. After all, it had a picture of the most adorable young girl ever to hit the cover—my daughter! What can I say? I'm a proud mom. But when I actually *read* the article, I felt embarrassed to be singled out as an exception. The overall tone and undercurrent of the article suggested that the women in our class had somehow failed by not going into the tech start-up world, that anyone who had chosen another path had missed out.

Hold on, I thought. Was this article really implying that the only yardstick for success for our entire class was how much money we made in tech? Is that *the* definition of success? Shouldn't we be asking different questions of ourselves, beginning with: Do you define success as happiness? Do you love your life and do what you love? Are you proud of your impact on your community? Do you live an authentic life? Are you able to ignore the voices of others who judge or diminish your accomplishments?

Aren't there as many ways to be successful as there are people? I think it's absurd that someone becoming a doctor or lawyer or artist or stay-at-home parent and community leader should feel like any less of a contributor to the world than the founder of a tech start-up. None of those roles or choices is any less of an accomplishment than that of someone who starts a company.

Of course, I'm all for equality and for women in tech and in business. No doubt we must work to close the many real gaps that still exist: the freedom gap, the wage gap, the backslide of women in STEM gap, the C suite, investor gap, and board seat gap. The stats are bandied about—women make 77 cents to the dollar earned by men; women need to work sixty extra days to make up for the loss of earnings caused by the gender pay gap. Millennial women show a smaller pay gap of 93 percent, but it doesn't last as they age and drop out of the workforce. In fact, recent studies show that more millennial women are planning on interrupting their careers than the previous generation.

All of these statistics are capped off by a trend I find even more troubling: In the last forty years, the happiness of women has been on the decline. That's right, since 1972, the year I was born, the United States government has been studying how happy we think we are, and every year women's happiness has declined. And women are less happy than men in spite of the many advancements in women's equality during those forty years. While no one can conclusively explain this decline, it certainly presents a "puzzling paradox": How can women have *more* choices and feel *less* happy? And why are they less happy than men?

Here's what I think is happening: Women have become less happy because somehow, with a broader set of choices, we feel a pressure to pursue work and family with equal fervor at all times. Then we suffer from the fear that we are not doing either well enough or worry about the judgment of others. Some of us fear that we are less of a mother if we choose to work outside the home. Others think we've squandered our hard-earned rights and our education if we are not climbing the corporate ladder.

More choices for women is hands-down a good thing. But accompanying that increase in options are more ways in which women can imagine failing or coming up short. If women fall into the trap of being guilt-ridden by both the choices they are making and the choices they are *not* making, then happiness is going to keep tanking.

Am I all for equal pay for equal work? Yes. Am I all for addressing the costs of early child care that can force many a young mother out? Yes. However, I am not for making other women feel inadequate and guilty, whether they decide to work on a career outside of the home or to work inside the home, focusing on child-rearing and home-making. Even well-meaning women can have a happiness-sucking, stinging impact on the guilt-ridden mind of a mom. Why? Because women have mastered guilt. Instead, we need to master happy.

You don't need to be a behavioral economist to know what happiness means for you. But be thoughtful about your own pursuit of happiness. Don't try to do it all or have it all. Aim to have what matters most to you, and only what you are consistently willing to work for. Don't diminish your joy by longing for the life that other people have chosen but that doesn't line up with what you truly want. Kick your guilt to the curb to make extra room in your life for joy.

I believe that defining our own happiness is key not just to raising female happiness, but to helping women achieve equality faster in the workplace. How can women lean in more if needless guilt and the judgment of others are constantly weighing them down and pushing them out? Sure, some of us should lean in, but many of us should also realize that it's fine to lean out if that's what we want—without feeling guilty about it.

don't be a mother judger

No conversation about women's guilt would be complete without a mention of the tension between working moms and stay-at-home moms. I am betting that you have many great, lifelong friends who chose to work outside the home as well as many others who have chosen not to. Your kids go to the same schools and play on the same sports teams. You get together for barbecues, couples dinners, and New Year's parties. You sit side by side at soccer games and back-to-school nights. But let's face it: behind this facade of community and friendship, there is some small part of you both—

Women have
mastered guilt.
Instead, we need to
master happy.

deep down, maybe even below the level of conscious awareness—that's judging the other for her choices and her lifestyle.

Let me ask you a serious question. When you see a woman with young kids who also has an accomplished, full-time career, part of you probably thinks, *You go, girl!* Right? But does another voice—a soft, almost abashed voice—also whisper, *Hmmm . . . those poor children. She must just be missing out on so much!*

Yes, men are child-rearing and taking on household duties more than they were a generation ago. But when they are at work, how often does someone ask a man, "Do you feel guilty leaving your kids at day care? Isn't it hard?" How many times has a man been traveling for work and been asked, "Oh, where are your kids? Who is taking care of them?" Probably zero. I, on the other hand, get asked this all the time. I used to have the urge to defend myself. I am a great mother! They are with their father! They are happy! Instead, I just deadpan, "Oh, I left them in the middle of the street, playing with knives."

You have to laugh, right? Like it or not, the battle lines have been drawn: working moms on one side versus stay-at-home moms on the other. But the question we need to ask ourselves here is: Why? Why have we turned on our friends and neighbors, strained our longest-standing female relationships, when what we really need to be doing is cheering on one another? Why have we entered into a perverse boxing match where the only outcome is that we *both* get beat up? Wouldn't it be better to hug it out than knock each other out? Instead of waging a lose-lose battle of mom versus mom, here is a better idea: let's truly respect each other's choices so we can *all* win when it comes to happiness.

Why do women judge other women? I think it's because we all make trade-offs in life, and when we do we can't help but resent what we perceive as the benefits and freedoms that would have come with the alternative choice. We can't have it all, but that doesn't stop us from wanting it and being a bit jealous of others having what we don't. The fact is that we are all looking at each other's "happy life" Facebook posts—whether it's news of a major job promotion, sweet moments playing at the park midweek, or blissful family vacation photos—thinking, *Hmmm . . . that must be nice!* forgetting, in that moment, the unique joy in our own personal choices. Instead of embracing the joy of our choices, we fall into the trap of guilt and old insecurities around them.

I believe that any direct or indirect judgment of others is deeply rooted in guilt and insecurity. That is why the topic of working versus stay-at-home moms hits such a raw nerve with many a mom. We are terrified that the trade-offs required by our choices are the wrong ones. Thus, we seek to silence our guilt, envy, and insecurity by making less than kind remarks about those who have made what we think are the opposite choices.

To the stay-at-home moms who think that working moms are looking down on them, I say this: sometimes when we look at you with what might seem like judgment, it's actually a pang of guilt or longing. Even if they love their jobs, all working moms long for the hugs that come with after-school pickup. When a working mom imagines a classroom mom getting to be a fly on the wall and watch her kid make a new friend, or sees a mom in workout gear at drop-off before she heads off to Spin class or lingers to socialize with other moms over coffee, that working mom is more likely jealous than judgmental.

Beyond this jealousy, though, it's impossible to overstate the respect and gratitude so many working moms have for the many stay-at-home moms who are active in their local schools and communities. They are doing more than their fair share, for the benefit of us all. Deep down, all working women know that we benefit from the community service of stay-at-home moms, and we are incredibly grateful for it.

To the women who work outside the home, keep doing it—guilt-free. If you want to focus full-time on an ambitious career in a way that a man would never be judged for or feel guilty about, go get 'em, tiger.

Everyone knows that staying home with young kids is wonderful but also demanding and tiring. That's why, when the weekend draws to a close, a lot of working moms, no matter how much they love their children, think *TGIM*—Thank God It's Monday! But being a working mom is not taking the easy way out and it does not make you less of a mother.

Feel proud that you can make it work for you and your family. Be proud that you pay critical tax dollars to fund public schools, that you continue to improve the workplace for women, and that you provide an alternative role model for all our daughters. Deep down, even a mother judger knows that she wants her daughter to see women kicking ass in a corporate setting just as much as she wants her daughter to know that it's also valid if she someday decides not to work and instead stay home and focus on raising her family. We are one tribe, but we are made better by our diversity of choices. So how can we support one another better? Be as thoughtful and kind as you hope your children will grow up to be. Comments such as "Are you just so busy working?" "It's too bad you can never make it to school!" "You know, we could really use your help in the classroom," and "Just ask the nanny, she's basically the mom" (even said about someone else), hit like a sucker punch. That's no kinder than saying things like "So now that you are not working, are you just eating bonbons all day?" and "You must be getting bored." That's below the belt of the stay-at-home mom, even if such comments are made half in jest. Of course we should continue to have real and honest conversations with one another, but a judgmental tone does not need to be a part of it. Other people pick up what you are laying down, even when you say it with a smile.

Women will make great strides in putting happiness on the rise only when we stop judging one another. At the same time, we'll all be much better off when we learn not to internalize the judgment of others, real or imaginary. What if, when you think you hear a judgmental comment, you assume positive intent and let it roll off your back? If you could, ask yourself: Is she being critical or simply curious? And if she did mean to be critical, is it because she is struggling with her own guilt or longing? Do I need to let this comment impact me? Does she get to vote on whether I am right in my own life? Whatever you do, don't lob back further judgment. Just put a stop to it.

Don't judge others, and don't be such a harsh critic of yourself.

If you are happy not working outside the home and you can afford not to, great! Your choice, your life. Your family unit does not owe it to society to have both you and your spouse "work." You are not letting womankind, or mankind, down. If you are in this situation, chances are you are a major contributor to your community, an invaluable asset to your kids' school, and a set of watchful eyes on the playground and in the neighborhood. You should never feel less than.

I know not just one but many stay-at-home parents ask themselves: Am I doing enough with my skills if I don't take a job outside the home and really go for it in my career? Is it enough to be *just* a mom? That is for you and only you to decide. And what about the women who decide to opt out of the traditional workforce even though they have the education and qualifications to be an executive? Are they wimping out—widening the gender leadership gap with their choices? Or are they simply following their own path to happy, which is their yardstick for success?

Once at a power women's breakfast in London, I met a managing director at a top investment bank. She confided to the group that she was miserable and wanted to quit to have more time with her family before her teens were out of the house. But she worried that she'd be letting down the younger women in her office, who always remarked that she was the only female at that level. She felt like she was taking one for the team, but it was making her miserable. She was successful in her career, but she felt unsuccessful in life. I think she owes more to herself and her family than she does to womankind. I just wanted to tell her to quit for a few years, soak them up, and then go back if she wanted to. She had been working for decades. When is enough, enough?

I know another woman who is not only an amazing wife and mother but also a community leader and champion for improving education for underprivileged children. Though her work is flexible and unpaid, it essentially adds up to a full-time job she puts in around her family's schedule. Yet, even though her choices benefit others and are extraordinary in their impact, she wonders if others judge her. When talking to former graduate school classmates who are working outside the home, she struggles with answering the question: "What do you do?" She feels embarrassed by the fact that she doesn't have a corporate email address and doesn't walk around with business cards. Yet in reality, she should feel proud that what she's doing for the community is benefiting those very classmates she feels judged by. Why do we feel like a company name needs to be in our email address to validate our impact? Why do we feel like part-time means we're wasting time?

If you want to embrace a career that allows your first priority to be flexibility, not dollars, feel great about that. If you want to get paid in hugs and kisses as much as in dollars, good for you. So what if a person who works differently at a different job gets paid differently?

It's not about who is more successful—it's simply about whether you are happy with the trade-offs that come with your choices.

it takes more than a village—it takes a tribe

Ours is still a transition generation: we want something very different for ourselves and our daughters than our grandmothers and mothers wanted for themselves and for us. And yet we are still feeling the influences of these women. I've told you about some of my influences. Heroic and amazing as she was, my grandmother still thought it was crazy that I would want to work after getting married, and I can't blame her—not working was a luxury for people of her generation, a sign of a good marriage. The reactions of your well-intended but perhaps outspoken mother or mother-in-law might be shaped by attitudes no longer shared by our generation. But you can't let your own choices be shaped by the outdated notions from generations past; instead, you need to look forward, toward the definition of success that fits *your* happiness.

It's up to us—our generation—to lift one another up, not compare, judge, or criticize one another's choices. Let's come together as one tribe and create a world in which alternative paths to happy are equally valued in the generations to come.

After all, we are not raising mini versions of ourselves—daughters destined to make the exact same life choices their mothers made. We want our daughters to pursue *their* dreams, not ours. Thus, we need to celebrate those showing them that there are many ways of being successful. Because, above all else, don't you want your children to be kind, healthy, and *happy*?

Raising confident and happy children doesn't just take a

We are all
one tribe,
made better
by the diversity
of traits and choices
among us.

village—it takes a tribe. I have so much love and gratitude for my tribe of female friends, and all they have done over the years to support me, in every way imaginable. My daughters will always know how much I value and respect these extraordinary women—which includes all the stay-at-home moms, the flex-work moms, and full time corporate moms—who I am lucky enough to call friends. I could have never made extraordinary happen in my life without the love and support of my girlfriends. And, I hope the daughters in our village will grow up never questioning whether a little girl can become a CEO and still be a good mom too. I hope they will be able to just take that choice for granted. To spark a group about how women can help lift other women up in your community, find a book club discussion guide at www.helloextraordinary.com.

One Extraordinary Tribe

- Give up the guilt. Being extraordinary isn't about doing it all; it's about doing all that matters. Guilt will only get in the way of your being the most extraordinary version of yourself you can be.
- Remember that a true partnership is one in which you take one another's burdens and make them half, and take one another's joys and make them double.
- Don't be a mother judger. Celebrate other women's choices for being just as valid as your own. And guess what? They are!
- Remember that we have the power and the privilege to create a better future for our daughters and granddaughters by showing that happiness *is* success, and that their way of being extraordinary is their own.

hello
extraordinary

A FEW YEARS AGO, WE WERE ON THE HUNT FOR A new house. Our girls were four and six, and we felt like our home was bursting at the seams.

After what felt like an eternity of looking, I went to see an old house that was walking distance from a great school for the kids and on the same street as the house of one of my best friends from college. I knew it needed some work, but it might just be perfect for us.

When we first went to see it, I took my first look around, and "perfect" did not come to mind. "Have we arrived at the House of Usher?" I was stunningly reminded of the Edgar Allan Poe story. Outside, the house was in a sad state of disrepair and overgrown with ivy. Faded curtains were drawn closed over every large, leaded-glass window. Paint was chipping, the stucco was cracked, and the shutters hung askew, ready to fall to the uneven pavement. My husband said, "Let's get out of here. There is no way we are buying this house!"

But we were there, so we figured we might as well go inside. Inside was worse.

The agent started telling us why remodeling would be *very*

difficult—potentially impossible. The house was historic, and thus protected, because Cecilia Casserly had lived there.

"Who?" I asked.

The agent went on to explain. From that conversation, and the historical report, we learned that Mrs. Casserly was an active and outspoken social reformer who had supported labor rights and women's rights. She was a major force in the American Red Cross during World War I and was awarded a medal of gratitude from France. During the 1918 flu epidemic, she had opened up the house to serve as a hospital to house more than fifty seriously ill patients in the very room I was standing in.

My husband looked at me nervously.

"You had me at suffragette." I smiled. We were home.

Suddenly, I didn't see the crumbling stucco. I could only see the legacy of a woman who had lived an inspiring, extraordinary life and who had the kind of extraordinary spirit that I dream of for myself and for my daughters.

There was no question that we would have to take the house down to its studs and rebuild it inch by inch. But with enough love, I knew we could turn it into the place our kids would grow up in until they became extraordinary women—and would one day maybe even bring home children of their own to visit us.

On the door frame that opened to the stairs to the attic, there were hundreds of notches marking the changing heights of daughters, sons, and cousins. The pencil and pen marks, rough scratches, and smudges were nothing short of a family's history that took over fifty years to create. As I ran my hand over the notches, feeling sad that this was going to be lost when we had to tear it out when we brought the house up to code, I became inspired to make sure the new stairs we built would say something special as a reminder of this remarkable history.

So I wrote a poem for our girls and had it painted on the treads of the new stairs. I hoped that every day, when they ran up the stairs to play, they would see what I wanted for them most in this life.

The poem is everything I believe in the core of my being. It is about how I have tried to live my life, and how I want my girls to live theirs. And how I hope, if you want to live extraordinary, you live yours.

step up

YOU HAVE ONE LIFE. STEP UP.
Create it with every step, every day.

FIND YOUR PASSION. THINK FOR YOURSELF.
Learn. Laugh. Listen.
Question.

SEE THE WORLD.
Dream. Dance. Sing. Create.
Be kind and forgiving.
Especially to your sister. Especially to yourself.
Be grateful, out loud, each day.
Embrace fear and failure.
It's the only way EXTRAORDINARY is made REAL.
If you want more, work more.
It will not come to you.

BELIEVE YOU CAN BEYOND REASON.

BE YOU. YOU ARE BEAUTIFUL exactly the way you are.
Know that no matter which way you go,

YOU WILL ALWAYS BE LOVED.
You will always be
my ☾ and my ☀
So don't wait for a magic elevator to your best life.

GO GET IT.
One step at a time.

no time like the present

Are you ready to leave ordinary behind? To say good-bye to the part of you that sees limits instead of possibilities? To the side of you that says no before yes? To the thought that extraordinary is only for someone else?

It's time. After all, that person isn't the real you—it never was. Life is just too short not to love what you do, why you do it, and who you do it with. And by the way, you won't miss ordinary.

So let's do a quick recap to remind you how ready you are to find your own extraordinary. Which area of your life do you want to focus on first? Refer back to the six P's, and start by picking a passion you want to ignite. Don't overthink it; just take the first steps along your path of action. Remind yourself to embrace the power of positivity; give yourself permission to ignore the naysayers, even the negative voices inside your own head. Commit to persevering on your path, never forgetting that those looking for easy never find extraordinary. And work smarter, not just harder. Focus on the ways to make yourself more productive, so that you can still find time to enjoy the other things that matter most to you along the way.

Will it take extra effort? You bet. The difference between ordinary and extraordinary is the extra you put in. Will it go exactly as planned? No, probably not. There are bumps on every road to success. Never want more than you are willing to work for, and never expect perfection. Get back up and get back to it. Lean on the positive people around you, and tap into a well of inspiration at www.helloextraordinary.com. Join the movement of people who are defining success as happiness and achieving more on their own terms.

Feeling inspired? Then pass it on by giving this book to someone else. After all, our greatest joys come not from what we create only for ourselves, but what we also share with others. That's what #HelloExtraordinary is all about: recognizing extraordinary in one another, inspiring others, celebrating choices different than your own, and expressing your gratitude— every single day.

So say hello to extraordinary. You'll find it's been there waiting for you all along.

acknowledgments

HERE'S THE THING I'VE LEARNED. WHEN YOU AGREE TO write a book, you have to write a book! Something I could not have survived alone. My hearty thanks and deep love to my guides along the way. To Talia Krohn, my fabulous editor at Crown. Had you not reached out, I would have never dove in. To Yfat Reiss Gendell, my fantastic agent, who guided this project with grace. To Billie Fitz-patrick, my writing partner, for the experience, talent, and attitude you brought to this book. And to Katie Sann and the entire Stella & Dot home office team, your support in this, as always, is greatly appreciated. And to our other team members at Crown, especially Megan Perritt, Ayelet Gruenspecht, Campbell Wharton, and Tina Constable, who have also contributed to making this book come alive.

To the tribe that is Stella & Dot. You are my muse. It was only when I knew I wasn't alone in my wants that I got the courage to create this life. Thank you for sharing your stories and giving me daily inspiration. It's that inspiration that I hope we can pass on to others with this book.

To my instrumental and inspiring early readers: Blythe, Mike, and Danielle. Thank you for invaluable feedback and stories. Thanks, as well, to my other early readers, including Tania Binder, Kim Matthews, Agatha Precourt, Erin Walhiem, Sharon Meers, and Andrea Higuera Ballard. Your thoughtful comments made this book so much better.

To my board of directors, for always putting our mission first.

To Alfred Lin and Leslie Blodgett, for their been-there-done-that wisdom. Your council is invaluable and has shaped my leadership for the better. Advice is great; empathy is even better. And no thanks could ever be enough to Doug Mackenzie, for being my longest standing linchpin. You have an extraordinary business mind, but even more important, you are an extraordinary person and an amazing friend with a generous heart. I have learned so much from you over these many years.

And a huge thank-you to my YPO Barbary Coast chapter mates. You are a phenomenal brain trust dedicated to being better leaders and all-around humans. Your perspective, love, and support have been essential. I've learned so much from you, and I hope it's been passed on in this book.

And thanks to my girls, for snuggling me while I wrote. And to Chad Herrin—my love, my partner, my rock, you didn't even go on strike after the second reading. Instead, you gave me your insights, and brought me tea and pudding so I could keep writing.

To my sister, Julie DiLullo Steele, who made sure I did not shame the family name by helping me think through the flow and tone of the book. So, if you don't like the book, you should definitely bring that up with my big sister. She did it!

And to my dad, Larry DiLullo, for his endless encouragement. I have no doubt that at least one person will buy several copies of this book.

index
....